ICON AND PULPIT

ICON
AND PULPIT

The Protestant-Orthodox Encounter

by
CARNEGIE SAMUEL CALIAN

THE WESTMINSTER PRESS
Philadelphia

2P19
C 128

181225

BOOK DESIGN BY
DOROTHY ALDEN SMITH

Published by The Westminster Press ®
Philadelphia, Pennsylvania

To the
WORLD COUNCIL OF CHURCHES
ON ITS
TWENTIETH ANNIVERSARY
(1948–1968)

Preface

We live in an age of dialogue. Protestants are talking to Roman
Catholics and Orthodox; Christians are speaking to Communists; Jews and Muslims are conversing with Christians; and
everyone is in touch with the secularists. Is this obsession with
dialogue merely peeking over fences or is it an authentic desire
to remove the fences that continue to separate us? Certainly,
we have improved upon our forefathers, who were more
polemically centered than we are; disputes rather than dialogue
characterized their day, creating fortresses with drawbridges
that clearly delineated the boundaries and differences. Today,
speaking across fences at least challenges us to consider removing these fences altogether. Such a step cannot be undertaken
lightly, nor can such a step be easily ignored by us or by our
children who will inhabit this shrinking world in the twenty-
first century.

Mindful of such a trend, I have addressed this book to those
who wish to think in terms of tomorrow's context, and more
specifically to Protestant and Orthodox Christians who have
been talking seriously since the embryonic stages of the ecumenical movement. The last twenty years of this dialogue have
been centered in the World Council of Churches. The intention
of this study is in part to review the dialogue that has transpired
over these years in order that it can serve as a platform for
further encounter in the context of the twenty-first century.

7

ICON AND PULPIT is intended to be more than an introductory study of Orthodoxy for a Protestant audience. There already exist several works introducing the life and thought of Eastern Christians, written by both Orthodox and non-Orthodox. This present study seeks to uncover a deeper level of encounter and to further current conversations in the light of tomorrow's demands.

Roman Catholics are also very much at the heart of all Orthodox-Protestant encounter. The reader will discover that the dialogue carried on in these pages involves all three of the major confessional divisions within the fellowship of Christian churches. Since Protestants and Roman Catholics share the same Latin, or Western, roots, this study seeks to serve purposefully the vital and mushrooming Protestant–Roman Catholic dialogue by revealing to Protestants that the full dimension of the catholicity, or universality, of the Christian faith can be realized only when sufficient attention is given to the Greek and Eastern roots of the church's heritage and development.

With the creation of numerous ecumenical courses in our universities, colleges, seminaries, and church programs, it is hoped that this book may find its place as a text through which students and churchmen may be stimulated to widen, deepen, and heighten the significant ecumenical engagements of this century.

While accepting full responsibility for the content of this study, I greatly appreciate the counsel of the many Orthodox scholars and churchmen who have been very gracious to me in my encounter with Orthodoxy. Unfortunately, all of them cannot be mentioned, but I thankfully acknowledge the encouragement given me in conversations with George Bebis, Georges Florovsky, John Meyendorff, Tiran Nersoyan, Nikos Nissiotis, Alexander Schmemann, Papken Varjabedian, Paul Verghese, John Yiannias, Nicolas Zernov, and the late Leon Zander. I also wish to express gratitude to many Protestants and Roman Catholics whose advice and counsel have been invaluable. Finally, to my faculty colleagues as well as to the librarians of our Associated Theological Faculties in Iowa I am indebted for their stimulation and cooperation, and also greatly value the time and opportunity that the Theological Seminary of the University of Dubuque has contributed to my preparation of this book.

Acknowledgment is also due to the editors of *The Christian Century, Worldview, The International Review of Missions, Theology and Life, The Ecumenist,* and *The Catholic World* as well as to the Commission on Ecumenical Mission and Relations of The United Presbyterian Church in the U.S.A. for permission to revise portions of my previous work as background within this present text.

This preface would be incomplete without tribute to my wife, who helped edit the manuscript; to Mrs. Elaine Weick, who typed it; and to the editors and staff of The Westminster Press, who efficiently handled its publication.

C.S.C.

Dubuque, Iowa

Contents

Part Three: SEARCH
FOR SPIRITUAL RENEWAL

Introduction

Rediscovery of Eastern Christendom is one of the most significant achievements resulting from the ecumenical climate of
the twentieth century. Largely silent in their suffering during
the past centuries, Eastern Christians have undergone both
persecution and proselytism under Islamic rulers and from
Roman Catholic and Protestant missionaries respectively. More
recently they have experienced pressures from communist gov-
ernments, and along with fellow Christians everywhere they
have been subjected to the stresses and challenges of the
secular city in an increasingly technological era that is changing
old behaviors and forming new ones. Within this age of changing attitudes and practices, Western Christians have shifted
from a suspicious and sometimes negative stance to an ecumenical and supportive role toward Eastern Christians. The goal
today is for cooperation and understanding among differing
Christian communities.

The Scope of Orthodoxy

Orthodoxy today is no longer limited geographically to the
East, but is worldwide in its scope. Although the origin of
Orthodoxy is strongly linked to the Mediterranean basin,
Orthodox Christians over the years have emigrated from the
East, so that today these believers can be found on the six
continents of the world and include within their ranks such

diverse peoples as Greeks, Russians, Ethiopians, Romanians, Poles, Albanians, Finns, Bulgarians, Japanese, Koreans, Chinese, Armenians, Egyptians, Syrians, Georgians, Yugoslavs, Indians, and Americans. Today there are Orthodox communities flourishing among the new African nations of Kenya, Tanganyika, and Uganda. Not to be overlooked are more than five million followers of these ancient churches in the Western hemisphere. In approximate figures there are 200 million Orthodox Christians in the world, 600 million Roman Catholics, and 250 million Protestants.

In America, the first Orthodox mission church was erected in 1794, on Kodiak Island in the Aleutians off the coast of Alaska. Shortly thereafter the Orthodox mission extended as far south as San Francisco. In more recent years, the steady influx of immigrants from Orthodox countries has led to a variety of national churches in North and South America with various degrees of dependence on their respective mother churches in their homelands. The Greek Orthodox Church is the largest single Orthodox jurisdiction in the United States. With the increased number of American-born members of these national churches, the dominant religious pluralities within the United States should be expressed in terms of Protestant, Roman Catholic, Jew, and Orthodox.

Before proceeding, let us define the term "Eastern Christian." "Eastern Christian" is the broad designation that covers the rich cultural and religious span of diversity found among these peoples. Eastern Christendom should never be treated as a monolithic whole, a common temptation for Westerners. These Christians are characterized by differences in racial, ethnic, and national backgrounds, while at the same time their origins are credited to the early apostles such as Thomas, James, Andrew, and Thaddaeus. The basic groups among Eastern Christians resulting from historic disagreements on political, social, and theological factors are the following: (1) the Byzantine Orthodox, or Chalcedonian, churches (including such groups as the Greeks and the Russians), (2) the Oriental

Orthodox, or non-Chalcedonian, churches (i.e., the Copts and the Armenians), and (3) the Eastern Catholic, or Uniate, churches in union with Rome (i.e., the Melchites and Maronites). We are concerned here primarily with the first two Orthodox groups, and will also briefly define the third.

Orthodoxy and the Council of Chalcedon

The basic separation between the Byzantine Orthodox (or Chalcedonian) churches and the Oriental Orthodox (or non-Chalcedonian) churches centers upon divergent opinions over the importance of the Fourth Ecumenical Council held at Chalcedon in A.D. 451. In the early life of the Christian church, ecumenical councils such as the one held at Chalcedon were summoned to discuss issues vital to the interests of the church universal. The recently adjourned Second Vatican Council viewed historically is not an innovation. The First Ecumenical Council was held at Nicaea (A.D. 325) under the leadership of Emperor Constantine. These councils brought together bishops, presbyters, and laity from different parts of the Empire.

The Fourth Council dealt with a dispute over the essential nature of Jesus Christ. It can be broadly stated that the theological declaration of the Chalcedon Council emphasized two distinct natures in Christ—divine and human—integrated within one person. The churches which disassociated themselves from Chalcedon (the Armenian, Syrian, and Coptic) felt that the mystery of Christ's nature should not be further analyzed beyond the explanations of the first three ecumenical councils. These non-Chalcedonian churches emphasized the one divine-human nature of Christ, in which both humanity and divinity are maintained in one person. In church history, an emphasis solely upon Christ's divine nature is called Monophysitism; this designation has unfortunately been attached to these non-Chalcedonian churches, suggesting that they denied Christ's humanity. This is not the case. On the contrary, it is not the denial of humanity but rather the unified and mysterious nature of Christ which these non-Chalcedonian churches advocated.

The controversy split the Eastern churches into two groups: those accepting the Council of Chalcedon, namely, the Greek Byzantine Orthodox churches; and the non-Chalcedonian, or Oriental Orthodox churches. Attempts are now being made to heal this historic wound, as witnessed by the unofficial consultation which convened at Aarhus, Denmark, in August, 1964, through the encouragement of the World Council of Churches. Such attempts at reconciliation among Eastern churches are similar to the experiences of churches in the West in this ecumenical era.

Eastern Rite Catholics

In addition to the above two groupings of Eastern churches, a smaller but significant third group should be mentioned in order to grasp the total diversity within Eastern Christendom. This is composed of the Uniate churches, more appropriately known as Eastern Rite Catholics, who are in union with Rome but maintain many of the indigenous religious customs and languages of their native lands. There is actually an Eastern Rite Catholic church serving as a counterpart to each of the churches in the Chalcedonian and non-Chalcedonian branches of Orthodoxy. This sometimes causes confusion for Protestants, who tend at times to link together Orthodox and Roman Catholics as being essentially the same. This is far from the case, even though there are areas that apparently overlap.

Orthodox Christians on the whole consider themselves almost as distant from Roman Catholicism as they are from Protestantism. Two of the basic differences between the Roman Church and the Orthodox churches are: (1) The latter do not acknowledge papal rule but hold to a conciliar form of government. Although both traditions have a hierarchy, allegiance to papal authority is not acceptable to Orthodoxy. Orthodoxy views authority in terms of freedom and decentralization. (2) There is also a difference of understanding regarding the Holy

Spirit as evidenced in each church's recitation of the Nicene Creed. (These differences will be amplified later.) Other items of variance can also be noted. The Orthodox, in contrast to the West, practice triple immersion in water as the baptismal act; the Orthodox use leavened bread in the Holy Communion, whereas the Roman Catholics do not; Baptism, Confirmation, and the Eucharist are administered to infants in Orthodoxy, but not so with Roman Catholics; Orthodox churches ordain married men, whereas Roman Catholics generally do not; the Orthodox do not have indulgence and purgatory as practiced by Roman Catholics. These differences and others should highlight the fact that Orthodoxy has a unique tradition, and any simplification or generalization would distort the picture of her unique place in today's ecumenical setting.

Part One

HISTORICAL ENCOUNTER

Chapter I

A Short History
of Orthodox-Protestant Relations

It would be wrong to suggest that Protestantism has discovered
Orthodoxy since the advent of the twentieth century. It is true
that today Orthodoxy is being recognized by Protestants more
than ever before, but it must not be overlooked that these two
divergent traditions have encountered each other earlier. Since
the inception of the Reformation, Reformed theologians have
sought affirmation of their precepts by looking to the ancient
tradition of the East. In the controversy between Rome and the
Reformers, the question was raised many times whether the
theological innovations in the West were unwarranted. "Conversely," as the learned Orthodox theologian Father Georges
Florovsky has asked, "was the Reformation really a return to
the doctrine and practice of the primitive Church, or was it a
deviation from it? In this debate the witness of the Eastern
Church was of primary importance."[1]

The Sixteenth Century and the Lutherans

The first recorded contact was initiated by Philip Melanchthon to Patriarch Joasaph II of Constantinople in 1559.[2] Sympathetic to the great suffering of the Eastern Christians under
Turkish rule, Melanchthon wrote to the Patriarch to express
the hope that in these last days Christian unity might be
realized, and to invite the Patriarch to accept Lutherans as
fellow Christians who honor the teaching of Scripture and the

early church fathers. However, Melanchthon's correspondence
was never acknowledged or answered. It has been speculated
that perhaps "it was delivered after great delay, already after
Melanchthon's death. What is especially interesting is that,
along with the personal message, Melanchthon sent the Patriarch a copy of the Augsburg Confession in Greek, obviously
as a proof of the doctrinal orthodoxy of the Lutheran communion."[3] Thus ended the abortive attempt at contact between
Wittenberg and Byzantine Christianity until 1573.

In 1573, under Protestant initiative, a young Lutheran theologian from Tübingen, Stephen Gerlach, was assigned as chaplain to the Imperial ambassador in Turkey, Baron David
Ungnad von Sonnegk. Gerlach carried with him letters from
fellow colleagues in Tübingen who wished to reopen correspondence with the Patriarch, who was now Jeremiah II. Gerlach also submitted another copy of the Augsburg Confession
in Greek for the Patriarch's consideration and comment. "A
hope was expressed that the Patriarch might see that there was
a basic agreement in doctrine, in spite of a certain divergence
in some rites, since the Protestants were not making any innovations, but kept loyally the sacred legacy of the Primitive
Church, as it had been formulated, on the scriptural basis, by
the Seven Ecumenical Councils."[4] The Patriarch's formal but
friendly reply disappointed Gerlach and his colleagues at
Tübingen.

The disappointment centered on the Patriarch's suggestion
"that the Lutherans should join the Orthodox Church and
unconditionally accept her traditional teaching. The Lutherans
persisted in their convictions. The correspondence went on for
some years and then broke off. In his last reply to Tübingen the
Patriarch simply declined any further discussion of doctrine.
Nevertheless, he was prepared to correspond in friendship.
And, in fact, he kept in touch with Tübingen for some time
after the formal termination of theological deliberations."[5] Thus
ended the first systematic and informal exchange between
Protestants and Orthodox.

Parenthetically, it should be noted that the irenic spirit expressed on both sides ironically also contained the seeds of increased tension between Lutherans and Orthodox. This was due to the unexpected publication of part of the correspondence through the ill-intended efforts of the Roman Catholic priest, Stanislaus Socolovius, who published it with editorial remarks under the thorny title *Censura Orientalis Ecclesiae: de praecipuis nostri saeculi haereticorum dogmatibus, etc.* This book received wide circulation by the Roman polemists who sought thereby to damage the reputation of Lutherans. This in turn forced the Lutherans to publish all the documents pertaining to the correspondence in both Greek and Latin with a defensive preface by the Lutheran theologian Martin Crusius under the title *Acta et scripta theologorum Wirtembergensium et Patriarche Constantinopolitani D. Hieremiae, quae utrique ab anno MDLXXVI usque ad annum MDLXXXI de Augustana Confessione inter se miserunt.*[6] This unfortunate involvement of Roman Catholics cast a shadow over the irenical beginnings of dialogue between Orthodox and Lutherans. However, it must be pointed out that the previous curtain of silence between these two divergent traditions had been torn.

The Seventeenth Century and Cyril Lucaris

The shadow of confusion and political intrigue continued to prevail into the seventeenth century in the case of Cyril Lucaris, the so-called Protestant Patriarch.[7] Lucaris was an intelligent and respected leader among his people, but one who was caught between the theological and political cross fire of Protestants and Roman Catholics in a non-Christian, Islamic setting. Lucaris, as ethnarch of the Greek Christians in Constantinople, desiring on the one hand to protect his community from Roman infiltration, and on the other, to free the Greek culture from Turkish influence, found himself involved in a struggle in which he was apparently willing to amend the tradition of his church in order to achieve favorable political and diplomatic ends for his people. The motivation and the sincerity of the man's true intentions continue even now to be questioned and debated by knowledgeable writers.[8]

Two points appear certain: first, that Lucaris was in need of Western help against the power of the Turks, and second, that Protestants rather than Catholics were favored by him as allies. Thus Lucaris cultivated his Protestant contacts beginning with the embassies of all the Protestant nations in Constantinople, especially the Dutch diplomat Cornelius Haga and the Calvinistic theologian Uytenbogaert. In addition to Calvinist influence, he became acquainted with British Ambassador Sir Thomas Roe, who put him in contact with the Archbishop Abbot of Canterbury; Lucaris later presented to King James I of England the famous Codex Alexandrinus of the Bible. The Anglicans in turn reciprocated with the gift of a printing press which saw some use before the Jesuits caused its demise. The Patriarch also sent his trusted deacon, Metrophanes Kritopoulos, to study at Oxford. Following the completion of his studies, he returned to Greece via Geneva, where he entered into further discussions with Reformed churchmen. During these conversations, Kritopoulos met the Piedmontese Antoine Leger, a Calvinist, who subsequently published in Geneva, in Latin, a work entitled *The Confession of Faith of the Most Reverend Lord Cyril, Patriarch of Constantinople, set forth in the name and with the consent of the Patriarchs of Alexandria and Jerusalem and other heads of the Eastern Churches*. This appeared in 1629 with almost simultaneous translations in French, English, and German, but the Greek text did not appear until four years later.[9]

Any intrinsic merit of the *Confession* was subordinated by the fact that it had become an obvious political instrument in the hands of Protestants in their battle against Roman Catholics. Conversely, it illustrated to the Roman Catholics the apostasy of the Greeks. "The sensation was immense. Here was one of the greatest Patriarchs of the Orthodox Churches of the East setting forth his faith in the authentic terms of Calvinism. The experts could recognize in the eighteen articles of the Confession the influence of the writings of Calvin himself, and of the *Confessio Belgica*."[10] Faithful and conservative Orthodox churchmen claimed that the *Confession* was a forgery. This claim, however, cannot be sustained; the original of the *Confession* is deposited in Geneva's Public Library. There is no doubt that Lucaris was influenced by Protestants and within a larger context was seeking Christian unity and *rapprochement*, but from a more immediate perspective was motivated by political considerations and therefore stood by passively as the Calvinist Leger exploited the situation politically for the Protestants within the polemical framework of that time.

The result was premature death for Lucaris. He was executed by the Sultan's Janissary Guards, with disguised encouragement from some Orthodox hierarchs and Jesuits. Once again, a shadow hung over Protestant-Orthodox relations, an air of falsity, which prevented whatever positive fruits might have materialized from the Lucaris episode. Lucaris' *Confession* was later condemned by a series of councils during the half century following his death (Constantinople, 1638; Constantinople, 1642; Jassy, 1642; Constantinople, 1672; Jerusalem, otherwise known as Bethlehem, 1672; Constantinople, 1691).[11] In short, his *Confession* provoked Orthodoxy's first historic confessional reaction to the Reformation.[12] According to Orthodox theologian Johannes N. Karmiris of the University of Athens, the *Confession* is "a Calvinist symbolical book written under Orthodox influence, rather than an Orthodox book written under Protestant influence. Were it not for a few Orthodox touches, anyone who did not know the author of the *Confession* would think that it was composed 'by Calvin himself or by one of his circle.' "[13] Lucaris' *Confession* did, however, perform a positive function for the Orthodox by forcing them to reflect upon the content of their theological thoughts.

Peter the Great—Late
Seventeenth and Eighteenth Centuries

During the latter half of the seventeenth century and into
the eighteenth, Protestant influence on Orthodox theologizing
was replaced by Roman Catholic influence. "Faced by the
inroads of Protestantism, Orthodox fought back with the
weapons that lay most readily to hand—Latin weapons."[14]
Rather than attempt to theologize within the authentic context
of her own tradition, she experienced a "pseudomorphosis,"[15]
avoiding the springs and roots of Orthodoxy itself. Not until
the nineteenth century would Orthodoxy begin to theologize
authentically again, departing from a defensive position of
trading Roman and Protestant arguments and setting them off
against each other.[16]

This period also witnessed the resumption of Lutheran and
Orthodox contact, but this time with Russians rather than
Greeks. The conversations centered around the person of Peter
the Great (1672–1725), who came, to a considerable degree,
within the spheres of both Lutheran and Anglican influence.
Already acquainted with many of the problems of the Reformation, Peter as emperor initiated ecclesiastical reforms which
in effect pointed to a "political Reformation."[17] He proclaimed
the emperor's ultimate authority over spiritual and temporal
affairs, a complete disregard for the symphonic doctrine of
church-state relations in Orthodoxy.[18] He negated canon law
and even had the approval of the Eastern Patriarchs in this
change, but it was most probably a coerced consensus, the
main factor being the sheer will and force of Peter's personality. Peter now felt that he was in a position to control and
initiate reform measures in the Orthodox Church of Russia.

Under Peter's reign, Theophanes Prokopovich was appointed Bishop of Pskov and introduced within the Russian
theological schools a kind of "Lutheran Orthodoxy"[19] as the
norm and content of teaching. A booklet appeared at this time
under the title *Ecclesia Graeca Lutheranizans.*[20] Also, the

Pietist center in Halle promoted Lutheran ideas in Russia. The royal marriage of Peter's son Alexius to a German princess furthered Lutheran influence in Russia, and Catherine II's religious instruction emphasized that there was no real difference between Lutheran and Orthodox doctrines.[21] In such an atmosphere it is not surprising that the true Orthodox understanding of the church became vague, losing its inner vitality. It is questionable whether any true encounter can take place when one of the partners in the encounter is lifeless.

The contact in the case of the Anglicans was begun by the British Nonjurors, a body of Anglican churchmen (including bishops, priests, and laymen) who had seceded from the Established Church and sought support and alliance for their position from the Orthodox.[22] Through a series of correspondences and conversations, a concordat[23] was accepted and favorably received by Peter, who acted as a mediator between the Nonjurors and the Eastern Patriarchs. The latter in the last analysis had to approve the reception of the Nonjurors into official fellowship. After a wait of two years, Chrysanthos Notaras, the Patriarch of Jerusalem, along with the other Eastern Patriarchs turned down the Nonjurors. Again, the Nonjurors, with Peter's encouragement, sent a second memorandum to the Patriarchs but nothing resulted, and further correspondence ceased.

It was clear that since the "heretical *Confession*" of Lucaris, the Eastern Patriarchs were still suspicious of all Protestants, including the Nonjurors, who had even written that they looked "forward to the day when the Liturgy of St. John Chrysostom will be sung in St. Paul's Cathedral. All practical problems can be settled later; unity in faith must be the beginning of everything."[24] In all these conversations the Anglicans deliberately avoided discussion of the validity of their orders and their acceptance by the Eastern Patriarchs. Father Florovsky has rightly observed: "This was not an accidental omission. We meet with the same omission time and again, from Jeremiah's correspondence with the Lutherans up to the middle of

the nineteenth century, when for the first time the doctrine of
the Church was brought to the fore in all ecumenical negotiations."[25] In other words, it is clear that political considerations
from the sixteenth to the nineteenth centuries received priority,
while theological considerations regarding the nature of the
church were subordinated. It is doubtful whether a real encounter did take place between Protestants and Orthodox
during these centuries, since true encounter necessitates an
honest confrontation with the problem of the nature and
doctrine of the church. Part Two of this book has for this
reason been limited to the crucial area of ecclesiology.

Nineteenth-Century Developments

The nineteenth century from the standpoint of Protestant-
Orthodox *rapprochement* was largely centered in the activities
of the Anglicans, reaching its high-water mark in the correspondence between William Palmer (1811–1879), a brilliant
deacon in the Anglican Church (who later submitted to
Rome), and Alexis S. Khomiakov (1804–1860), a lay theologian in the Russian Church and author of the famous essay
The Church Is One.[26] Other significant figures during the century were, on the Orthodox side, Philaret (1782–1867), brilliant Metropolitan of Moscow who envisioned a mystical unity
of the church universal, and in the second half of the century
the illustrious philosopher Vladimir Soloviev (1853–1900).
Among the Protestants was Edward B. Pusey (1800–1882),
who worked along with Palmer through the Tractarians, a
movement on the part of some Anglicans to make the "catholic" conception of the church once more central in Anglicanism, reflecting upon the apostolic continuity of the Christian
church.

Philaret, considered the greatest theologian of the Russian
Church in modern times, wrote *Conversation of a seeker and a
believer concerning the truth of the Eastern Greco-Russian
Church,* amid the political world of the Holy Alliance (1815)

under the three-way imperial rule of an Orthodox Russian, a Lutheran Prussian, and a Catholic Austrian.[27] In other words, there was already an effort toward a political unity of Christendom, which created an almost compulsive climate among churchmen of the respective traditions to create a spiritual unity. Toward this end, the first quarter of the century saw the realization of the founding of the Russian Bible Society with the cooperation of various churches in Eastern Christendom. The Bible was recognized as one common and authoritative medium throughout Christendom.[28] However, some Orthodox felt that the "Bible enthusiasts" were promoting a brand of Western Pietism; and the Bible Society was therefore disbanded by order of the government in 1826.

Philaret himself was educated in Orthodox schools that were heavily influenced by Protestant categories of thought, but instead of becoming a cryptic Protestant, he translated his insights into his indigenous Orthodox context. The outside sources actually worked positively upon him to enlarge his theological vision and to alert him more fully to the unity of Christendom and the present fact of disunity. His education in Protestant thought reinforced his anti-Roman bias toward Scholastic theologizing, but did not keep him from developing a respect for the traditions of the past. He held the office of Metropolitan of Moscow for forty-seven years, a sufficient span of time to leave his imprint upon the Russian Church of the nineteenth century.[29]

It was during Philaret's reign that Khomiakov and Palmer carried on the correspondence and visits which also involved Pusey and the Tractarian movement. Palmer and Pusey were among the chief spokesmen for the movement. Khomiakov contended that more than doctrinal agreement between the Anglicans and Orthodox was needed. Unity for him was greater than the sum total of common doctrines. Rather, he sought for "an inner unanimity, a 'common life' in the Catholic Truth. 'Unions' are impossible in the Orthodox Church; there can be only 'Unity.' This 'Unity' has been broken: the West separated itself from the unity, i.e., acted as a self-contained entity. It was a violation of Christian love, a substitution of the particular for the universal. Unity can be restored only by the return of those who went their own way, instead of abiding in it originally. This was just the opposite of what Palmer contended."[30] The issue between them was clearly drawn.

With an increase in theological conversations between the confessions, Roman Catholics as well as Anglicans initiated organizations and publications, sharing the Tractarian[31] concern for catholicity. For example, Johann Adam Moehler (1796–1838), professor of church history on the Catholic Faculty of Tübingen, viewed the church as a living organism rather than as an institution.[32] Abbé Guettée, a French priest who became a convert to Orthodoxy, founded a magazine called *L'Union Chrétienne,* dedicated to the cause of reform and reunion, probably one of the earliest ecumenical publications. Joseph J. Overbeck, member of the Theological Faculty at Bonn, was another convert from Catholicism to Orthodoxy, and was an early spokesman for an "Orthodoxy of the Western Rite," somewhat parallel to the "Catholicism of the Eastern Rite."[33]

On the Anglican side, John Mason Neale's historical studies and translations of the Eastern liturgical texts did a great deal to expand communication and understanding (*The History of the Holy Eastern Church,* 5 vols., 1847–1873). The visit of W. J. Birbeck, an Anglican layman, as well as numerous prelates, encouraged dialogue between the two traditions. Various groups were formed to express interest in Orthodoxy: The Association for the Promotion of the Unity of Christendom (1857); The Eastern Church Association (1863); The Anglican and Eastern Orthodox Churches Union (1906; American branch, 1908). The latter two organizations were fused in 1914 under the name of "The Anglican and Eastern Churches Association." From the Orthodox side, the Society of the Friends of the Anglican Church was inaugurated in St. Petersburg in 1912.

Finally, there is the Fellowship of St. Alban and St. Sergius founded in 1928.[34]

Nevertheless, in spite of the many friendly contacts and joint publications, decisive divisions between the two confessions remained as observed by the wise Philaret during the first half of the nineteenth century. These divisions continue as Anglicans and Orthodox resume their conversations today, seeking to compose a new chapter in their relations with one another in our century. In Philaret's opinion any *rapprochement* between the two churches must consider (1) the will of the people (more than an act of the hierarchy); (2) the validity of Anglican orders (this question also pertains to the other Protestant churches from an Orthodox viewpoint); (3) the implications inherent in the Thirty-nine Articles and their doctrinal content; (4) the Filioque clause in the Nicene Creed which remains objectionable to the East; (5) the definition of apostolic succession; (6) the place of tradition in relation to Scripture; and (7) the entire sacramental structure of the church beginning with the Eucharist.[35] Clearly, Metropolitan Philaret's observations and reservations are as contemporary today as they were a century ago in the dialogue between these two churches.

In discussing the nineteenth century, we must add a further word concerning Vladimir Soloviev (1853–1900), the Russian philosopher who, like Philaret, envisioned a mystical and universal church. While Philaret's orientation contained an anti-Catholic bias, Soloviev had an anti-Protestant bias. "Soloviev was mainly concerned with the question of reconciliation between the East and Rome, and in a sense he was pleading for a very particular kind of 'Unia.' In fact, he simply did not believe that 'Churches' were separated. There was an historical estrangement, an external break, but, in an ultimate sense, there was still One (mystically) Undivided Catholic Church."[36] Father Florovsky considers Soloviev's basic vision to be correct; namely, that the church is an integral whole and conse-

quently cannot be divided. "Either Rome is no Church at all,
or Rome and the East are somehow but One Church, and
separation exists only on the historical surface. This thesis can
be interpreted in a limited sense, i.e., as including only Rome
and the Eastern Orthodoxy. But it could be reinterpreted in a
wider sense, and, in that case, we would have an important
and truly ecumenical plea."[37] Soloviev's mature ecumenical
vision was finally expressed in his famous *Short Story of the
Antichrist*,[38] which included Protestants along with Catholics
and Orthodox. The vision depicts a discussion of the three
traditions in the symbolized figures of Dr. Pauli, who represents the intellectual honesty of Protestants, Pope Peter, who
maintains the value of authority, and Orthodoxy's Elder John
with his devotional and spiritual insights. Together these
symbolized personages highlight the three presuppositional
pillars necessary for a truly *catholic* comprehension of the
Christian church.

The Twentieth Century and the World Council of Churches

Even in the second half of the twentieth century, Soloviev's
ecumenical vision of unity remains distant, but the ways and
means of communication and technology have improved significantly since the days of Melanchthon. The ease of contact
between East and West has led to greater and more frequent
involvement. Orthodox theologian Father John Meyendorff
has rightly commented that "the historical estrangement of
East and West, linguistic, spiritual, intellectual, is bound to
disappear in a world which becomes too small. The 'non-
theological' elements of our estrangement will soon belong to
the past. Orthodoxy today is no more—and will become less
and less—an 'Eastern' Church, just as Western Christianity
ceases to be only 'Western.' This will help us to forget the
relative issues and concentrate on the real ones."[39] Thus the
challenge comes to Protestants in unequivocal terms from the
largest single confessional group within the World Council of

Churches. Indeed, the World Council has made an important shift from being a largely Protestant-engineered forum to a viable interconfessional gathering of more truly pan-Christian character. Long strides have been made since the issuance of that now famous encyclical by the Ecumenical Patriarchate in 1920.[40]

The membership of Orthodoxy in the World Council of Churches has saved the Council from a more limited role as a pan-Protestant organization. At the same time, Orthodoxy's presence has made deliberation and progress slow, with mis-understandings at times outweighing areas of understanding. Churchmen in either tradition are aware of the situation, but the benefits gained have more than offset the risks taken. The present danger is that ecumenicity may become associated with uniformity rather than with nobler goals of unity and community of churches. To maintain a worthy witness before each other requires keener awareness of the unique nature of one's own tradition; it also requires more than pleasantries with one another in ecumenical gatherings.

Effort must be exerted on both sides to understand the categories of thought and expression in each other's formulations. For the Protestants, this at least implies a working knowledge of the patristic period discussed in the next chapter. For the Orthodox, according to Father Alexander Schmemann, this means that "the Orthodox must make the firm affirmation that in any ecumenical encounter . . . the Orthodox Church is always and by her very nature the other 'half' standing together *with,* and yet always *against,* the totality of the Protestants."[41] This similar spirit must be maintained by Protestants toward the Orthodox, for it is only out of the fullness of each tradition that authentic witness and exchange of insights can take place between these "ancient" and "younger" churches as they proclaim together the mysteries of our one faith revealed in Jesus Christ.

Chapter II

The Greek Patristic Tradition:
A Common Heritage

Most Protestant churchmen of today are ignorant of the patristic period in church history. Protestant scholarship is first preoccupied with the church of the New Testament, and then
steps into a mysterious "time tunnel" that misses the interven-
ing centuries until serious study resumes again with the Reformation.[1] Anglican scholars are an exception to this sweeping
statement; concentrated theologizing for many of them is centered upon the first five centuries of Christian history. Roman
Catholics are less ignorant than Protestants regarding the
church fathers. Catholics are generally well versed in the Latin
patristic literature, but share with Protestants a surprising gap
concerning the Greek fathers who preceded the Latin fathers
by at least one hundred years. Even today, the importance
attributed to Augustine by the Latin West is not shared by the
Greek East;[2] despite the opposition of Ecumenical Patriarch
Photius (A.D. 895), Augustine was removed from the Orthodox
calendar of the saints as a heretic. As a result the East has not
shared the Augustinian orientation of the West.

Today's ecumenical conversations between the East and
West reflect this theological ignorance of the patristic period.
This became extremely clear at the Fourth World Conference
on Faith and Order in Montreal (July, 1963), where references
to the church fathers abounded as never before at an ecumenical gathering. The future will no doubt substantiate the statement that any partner in dialogue "who proposes to talk unity

without knowing his Irenaeus or Cyprian or Augustine may soon be in the situation of the man who can dive but cannot swim."[3] It seems clear to this writer that the period of the fathers, largely unexplored by the contemporary churchman because of its supposed "irrelevance," holds great promise as ground for possible doctrinal unity among Christians. This is especially true for the Greek patristic literature, which is the oldest universal language of the Christian church.[4] It can be stated that the Greek fathers expressed a common heritage of catholicity for the church, even in its diversity, exhibiting a spirit that has since been unmatched in Christian history.

Rediscovery of Our Pre-Reformation Roots

The life of the church in the early centuries was Greek oriented before Latin influence was felt. It should be noted that in these early years there was a constant stream of intellectual and spiritual stimulus flowing from East to West, whereas there was no comparable counterflow from West to East. Orthodoxy remembers this past with pride, and reminds the West of this in every mutual encounter. De-Westernization of the World Council of Churches, a concern expressed by General Secretary of the World Council of Churches Eugene Carson Blake, can take place in a profound way by a working knowledge of the Greek fathers in the theological formulations of the World Council.[5]

A theological shift to the problems and formulations of the Greek fathers might serve as a healthy corrective for the current impasse surrounding unresolved "Faith and Order" issues dealt with predominantly from Western presuppositions and methods of theologizing. For Protestants and Orthodox in the World Council, such an exploration into the field of historical theology might prove mutually illuminating, encouraging each side to examine this common body of Christian heritage freshly from a shared desire for unity. Such an experience will no doubt release some Orthodox from long held opinions regarding particular teachings of the fathers as they discover some teachings to be based upon proof texts. Protestants can be understanding at this point, in view of their own history of proof-texting from Scripture. In spite of such possibilities, the significant point to observe is that both partners in dialogue will be dealing with a common body of material which existed when the Christian church experienced more unity than it does today.

Florovsky has expressed this need for a rediscovery of pre-Reformation roots in his proposal for a "neopatristic synthesis," which means primarily a study of the fathers from the fourth through the eighth century. He wishes to supplement the Western accent upon "ecumenism in space" with an Eastern accent upon "ecumenism in time." "We have to examine," he says, "the existing tensions and divergences with a prospective synthesis in view. I mean exactly what I say: a synthesis and integration, and not just a toleration of the existing varieties of particular views. No ultimate synthesis is possible in history but still there is a measure of integration for every age. Our fault is precisely that we are behind the times, behind our own time. We have to recognize the common ground that existed a long time ago. This seems to be the most imposing ecumenical task."[6] Orthodoxy, Florovsky believes, is the guarantor and promoter of "ecumenism in time," in contrast to geographical "ecumenism in space" advanced by Protestants in the ecumenical movement.[7]

From the viewpoint of "ecumenism in time," the patristic period is an extension of and synonymous with the apostolic era. Florovsky contends that the apostolic and patristic roots of the Christian church cannot be separated. "Only by being 'Patristic' is the Church truly 'Apostolic.' "[8] The church fathers theologized in the manner of the apostles and not in the spirit of Aristotle. It is the Aristotelian influence in Thomistic theology that Orthodoxy rejects.[9] Patristic theology can be described as existentially rooted in the decisive commitment of faith. "In the age of theological strife and incessant debates, the great Cappadocian Fathers formally protested against the use of dialectics, of 'Aristotelian syllogisms,' and endeavored to refer theology back to the 'vision of faith.' Patristic theology could be only 'preached' or 'proclaimed'—preached from the pulpit, proclaimed also in the words of prayer and in the sacred rites, and indeed manifested in the total structure of Christian life. Theology of this kind can never be separated from the life of prayer and from the exercise of virtue."[10] Theology seen in this light is but a *means* to acknowledge the mystery of the living God; it is not a theology of rules, regulations, and dogmas per se. For example, the "Christological formulas are fully meaningful only for those who have encountered the living Christ, and have received and acknowledge Him as God and Saviour, and are dwelling by faith in Him, in His body, the Church. In this sense, theology is never self-explanatory discipline. It is constantly appealing to the vision of faith."[11] To be aware of this theological attitude is to recover the spirit of the "patristic mind" and with it a recognition of pre-Reformation roots for Protestants who are in search of an ecumenical tradition that expresses both continuity and Biblical content.

Importance of the Greek Fathers in Retrospect

Who were these church fathers who have extended the apostolic tradition of the church? There will be no attempt to give an exhaustive list of the fathers or to suggest that the fathers are limited to certain centuries. In fact, there are views within Orthodoxy which insist that the period of the fathers must be seen in an open-ended way, which would include such later Byzantine theologians as St. Simeon (the eleventh century) and St. Gregory Palamas (the fourteenth century).[12] For our purposes, an arbitrary time period from the second to the fifth century has been selected to denote some of the dis-

tinguishing characteristics among the Greek fathers of which
an ecumenically minded Christendom should be aware in these
days of converging traditions.

Justin the Martyr is considered one of the first among the
patristic fathers, the first theologian and philosopher who stood
within the apostolic tradition amid a Hellenistic culture. He
saw his role as a secular missionary to a Hellenistic environment. Justin was optimistic about the harmony of Christianity
and Greek philosophy.[13] Justin would conceivably be much in
sympathy with today's preoccupation with philosophical theology.[14] For him, "Christianity was philosophical truth itself;
Plato was, in his estimation, already very largely in agreement
with the truth of Christianity."[15] Justin saw the footprints of
God in the non-Christian order and in nature. Socrates for him
was a Christ-type individual. Justin's "Christ is a philosopher,
'no sophist,' but a genuine teacher of the way to 'happiness'
(*eudaimonia*), in himself the personification of 'right reason'
(*orthos Logos*) teaching 'divine virtue.' His teaching in the
Sermon on the Mount is wholly in line with natural law; it is
a universal morality, valid for all races and stripped of the
national particularism of Judaism."[16] For Justin, there is an
essential harmony and oneness between Christ and the highest
Reason of the Platonist. Hence, the two major barriers preventing conversion for him were prejudice and misinformation
regarding Christians.[17]

From Justin's concern with the philosophic context of Hellenistic culture, we move on to Irenaeus who was preoccupied
with the embryonic forming of a canon. While Marcion defined the contents of the canon negatively, Irenaeus gave it a
positive structure. He was the first to set consciously the canon
of the four Gospels as the beginnings of the New Testament
and to declare the standards necessary if a writing was to be
included. As the earliest literary theologian and canonist of
the Christian church, he rejected the apocalyptic writings of
the Gnostics. The conscious formation by the church of a canon
should underline for Protestants the fact that the Bible is a

product of church tradition.[18] This has been an issue upon which Orthodox and Roman Catholics have long insisted, and only recently, in this age of convergence, have Protestants come to appreciate the point without having to surrender their Biblical concern.

Irenaeus was followed by Clement of Alexandria, who was largely influenced by the Platonic synthesis developed by Justin. Like Justin, he was much in contact with the culture of his day. Clement sought to meet the demand of thinking Christians with a more coherent account of their faith. He viewed philosophy as a preparatory study for theology, the grammar necessary for structured theological inquiry. His writings in the *Protrepticus,* or "Exhortation to Conversion," the *Paedagogus,* or "Tutor," and the *Stromateis,* or "Miscellanies," contain flashing insights with many practical suggestions for the Christian life. He saw faith as an intuitive inward testimony to the highest and best, a capacity for recognition.[19] He always insisted that truth be judged by what is said, not by who says it.[20] The Scriptures for him were basically the story of God's narrative to educate humanity back to himself, "sometimes by severity as in the Flood and other miracles, but throughout acting with the purpose of love which has its pre-eminent manifestation in the incarnate Lord."[21] He thought it wrong to regard celibacy as a state inherently nearer to God than the married state, "as if sexual intercourse involved a ceremonial or moral defilement. In fact, the married man has greater opportunities for sanctification than the celibate, since he faces the daily exasperations that come to him from his wife, his children, and his household responsibilities."[22] The contemporary mood highlights the freshness of his views, which cannot be denied by Protestants (or Roman Catholics either) who have previously imputed stuffiness to church fathers such as Clement.

Origen stands out as perhaps the earliest Bultmannian in the life of the church. He felt that the unhistorical conceptions of the Bible made it necessary to develop an allegoric kind of

exegesis as an explanation. His theologizing was later regarded
as rather unorthodox, but his stimulation and consequent enrichment of other Christians cannot be denied. Origen saw the
need to state formal creedal propositions in an unqualified and
dogmatic form for the church's essential continuity. However,
beneath these affirmations, he possessed a lively spirit of investigation and speculative inquiry which was contagious
among those who heard his teachings or read his works.[23]
Origen was aware that there was great danger in having over-
confidence in theological matters. In theological speculation,
he felt that absolute confidence was possible for only two
classes of people, saints and idiots.[24]

The inclusion of Origen in any list of the church fathers
should make us quickly aware that the Greek fathers, like the
Orthodox churches, cannot be treated as a monolithic and
"orthodox" whole. To the uninitiated, reference to the fathers
often suggests the absence of heresy, the advocacy of "right
belief." This is not necessarily the case as we begin to see that
some fathers are more "orthodox" than others and that the
norms or standards by which "right belief" is determined are
not fixed, something that is not always clearly expressed by
Orthodox churchmen in ecumenical encounters. Certainly the
fathers enjoyed a common vision of faith which served as the
essential norm of their theologizing, but their understanding
of that vision resulted in a rich diversity of expressions. Would
it not be more accurate to state, then, that there is more than
one way to interpret God's revelation, and that we are all subject to seeing through a glass darkly, though some may be able
to see from the past and in the present through that glass a bit
more clearly than others?

Eusebius of Caesarea followed Origen, and the major emphasis changed this time from philosophy to philology—a crit-
ical examination of the Biblical foundations and language of
Scripture. He became the earliest church historian. He saw the
need for translating the finality of Jesus Christ into a context
and vision of universal history.[25] His work *Ecclesiastical His-*

tory addressed itself to the finality and universality of Jesus Christ. He demonstrated that "Christianity and Christ possessed great antiquity, and the history of Christianity was a universal history."[26] Eusebius gave much effort in his study to the history of heresy, since for him dogma was fixed and permanent. Dogma was not subject to historical development; "it was only heresy that developed, and therefore only heresy that had a history in this sense of the word."[27] His distinction between dogma and heresy reminds us in an ecumenical era that faithfulness to a church's tradition can be traced to a process of development. If the nature of heresy is developmental, then are not the dogmas of our respective traditions under the judgment of God's revelation—the dogma of God? Eusebius' concern is essentially an apologetic for the Christian faith; his theology of history conditions and influences him as a historian. Above all, his vision to present the finality of Jesus Christ within the context of universal history gives a permanent value to his work for all ages.

Athanasius followed Eusebius and was chiefly responsible for the church's acceptance of the Nicene-Constantinopolitan Creed, the hallmark of Orthodoxy. He also developed monasticism in the life of the church. Athanasius was more than a Christian philosopher and theologian; he was preeminently a churchman par excellence. "Athanasius was the first Greek Father of the Church who was not at home in the academic atmosphere of Christian philosophy. He was a 'Churchman' who was also well versed in theological matters, but he was trained in the administration of the Alexandrian hierarchy. His spiritual home was the divine service and the administrative desk in the ecclesiastical office, not the school platform."[28] Theology was primarily a weapon to oppose heresy, especially the Arians. Salvation from death[29] and the life-giving fellowship with God are his central themes. "The greatness of Athanasius was his single-minded and undeviating conviction that Christianity was a religion of salvation, and his refusal, even and especially in the conflict over the person of Christ, to regard as theologically essential any notion that could not be closely related to the theme of salvation."[30] Jesus Christ is for him *the* Light of the World who has come to illumine the darkness of our existence.[31] Light is one of the key images developed in his writings to defend orthodox belief against Arianism. The theme of light continues to our day to be an admirable confession of faith in Jesus Christ, for is it not at the core of Christian belief that only in the light of Christ do we have the promise of guidance for our lives?

A generation after Athanasius, Basil the Great sought, like Justin, Clement, and Origen, to formulate a synthesis between philosophy and theology. The result was a Neoplatonic metaphysics. He distinguished himself as the first great example of the monk who became bishop, the ideal of Orthodoxy. He felt bishops should be spiritual giants first and administrative experts secondarily. He was also a social reformer; he might even be referred to as the early Rauschenbusch of the Christian church. Finally, he was the initiator of the formal sermon in Greek; he strove to emphasize the real purpose of all theology as that of leading the faithful to spiritual composure and adoring praise of the mystery of God. He wrote extensively on the divinity of the Holy Spirit (*De Spiritu Sancto*) and went beyond Athanasius in discussing "the Trinity of the 'Hypostases,' the segregating peculiarities of which do not destroy the unity and completeness of the divine Life."[32] Today we seek to give greater recognition to the Spirit, to balance theology's previous and extensive theologizing on the Father and the Son; thus what Basil and the church fathers have to say on the Spirit will be of extreme importance.[33]

The next two fathers, along with Basil the Great, are commonly referred to as the "great Cappadocians." Basil was the outstanding figure, and Gregory of Nazianzus and Gregory of Nyssa completed the trio. The latter two were actually brothers and served as friends and collaborators of Basil.[34] Nazianzus (known in the Orthodox Church as Gregory the Theologian) and Nyssa developed further the mystical outlook of Orthodox theology. Nyssa in particular was responsible for furthering the concept of *theosis* ("deification"), or "sanctification," to be discussed in later chapters. It should be pointed out here that Nyssa's concern for *theosis* reveals that he was deeply moved by the problems of man. "The realization of salvation, the elevation and transformation of the individual, the relation to the life of the body and the survival of the soul after death—these are problems to which he returns again and again, however circuitously."[35] Nyssa's concern for the interior life of man revealed his psychological and pastoral astuteness, which are also areas of great concern today.

John Chrysostom and two of the Cappadocians, Basil the Great and Gregory of Nazianzus, are recognized by the Orthodox as the "Three Hierarchs." They are considered the ecumenical teachers of the church.[36] Chrysostom distinguished himself as *the* preacher among the Greek fathers and is best known to the majority of the Orthodox through his liturgy, which is regularly celebrated in Orthodox (Byzantine) churches. Chrysostom "was the prototype of the Churchman who remains loyal to his spiritual mission to the end and who would think it treason to have any regard for political circumstances and the powerful of this world."[37] Even though he was a victim of political and ecclesiastical intrigue, and was removed as the Bishop of Constantinople, dying in exile, the injustice done to him was recognized posthumously and his remains were interred in the Church of the Holy Apostles in Constantinople (A.D. 438). To this day, his homilies are read in the West as well as the East. His sermons "reflect something of the authentic life of the New Testament, just because they are so ethical, so simple, and so clear-headed."[38] Chrysostom is as much a "father" of the church today as he was then.

The last father to be considered in our series is Cyril of Alexandria, who is "the most distinguished saint of Byzantine orthodoxy."[39] No one before Cyril emphasized the importance of the preceding fathers, placing them for all practical consideration on a par with Scripture. By setting the pattern in

this manner, he was the first Byzantine Scholastic theologian
to establish Scripture plus the preceding fathers as the basic
norm in the life of the Christian church. Cyril opposed Nes-
torius by establishing the term *Theotokos* (God-bearer) over
Christotokos (Christ-bearer) in reference to Mary, thus enhancing her early veneration in the Orthodox (and Roman
Catholic) churches. Above all, his practice of quoting from
the preceding fathers, especially Athanasius, became the "orthodox" way of doing theology. While there is obvious merit
in referring to the fathers as historic signposts in theologizing,
the practice started by Cyril has restricted and undermined
the theological vigor and ardor of Orthodox theology to the
extent that it has become known derogatorily in our day as
merely a "theology of repetition."[40] Protestants, no less than
Orthodox (and Roman Catholics), are also subject to this
pattern of decay if today's theologizing is no more than a quoting of familiar names such as Barth, Brunner, Niebuhr, Bult-
mann, Tillich, Bonhoeffer, and others among our twentieth-
century "church fathers." Of course, the Basils and Gregorys
as well as the Barths and Niebuhrs must be known and even
mastered as reflections of the church's consciousness in their
day. Their thoughts stimulate and free us to become theologians for the emerging consciousness of tomorrow's church.

Theologizing in the Spirit of the Fathers

Has a steadfast adherence, then, to the tradition of the
fathers, promoted by Cyril, suffocated and weakened Orthodox theology? Professor von Campenhausen suggests that it
has. "The Fathers had become so holy that in the end they
could no longer beget any sons who were their equals in
vitality. . . . Imprisoned in their own territorial and cultural
confines, their Church rested upon its own perfection. It
trusted in an unchanging and indestructible continuity with
the apostles and Fathers of the past whose achievements it
admired so much that it failed to observe the changing nature

of the problems which faced theology. It preserved their intellectual inheritance without doing anything to renew it."[41] Orthodoxy, like post-Reformation Protestantism, has suffered from a scholasticism that has undermined its theological vitality. However, a patristic scholasticism as such does not negate the inherent and healthy spirit of theologizing found in the fathers.

The essential and abiding spirit contained in the theological statements of the fathers includes: (1) Their attitude of worship and reverence before God, for they were extremely conscious of God's unapproachableness. They reflected the Hebrew sentiment that the name of God must not be uttered. Thus in their understanding of God and propositions about him, there was always a sense of incompleteness, a spirit of silence.[42] (2) The fathers' strong adherence to the Holy Spirit as the Revealer of what can be known by man about God. Irenaeus insisted that statements about God must be revealed by God through his Spirit. It is only in the Spirit that truth about God can be apprehended, and even then the revelation is not without its mystery. Mystery will always surround the glory of God. Along with the spirit of silence, then, is this majestic spirit of glory and awe in the theologizing of the fathers influenced by their dependence upon the Holy Spirit. A consequence of this is the keen awareness of man's limited capacity for divine comprehension. (3) The fathers' consciousness that any human means of expression regarding the theological mysteries of God and the universe would be restrictive in nature. For example, "It would be inherently wrong to use expressions like 'right hand' or 'bosom' or even 'father' and 'son' as if they meant when applied to God the same thing they mean when used of creatures."[43] The danger is always there in theological statements of speaking in *human* terms of God and then dogmatizing upon these terms.[44] "This was one of the major issues in the Arian controversy, for the Arians fell into error by refusing to admit the limitations of creaturely images and notions, and by pressing them improperly into use beyond their creaturely reference, and so they distorted the knowledge of God through the misapplication of human and earthly analogies."[45] Thus the conscious spirit of the fathers on the limitations of all human efforts in theologizing is a salutary one not to be overlooked by us today.

Taking these patristic characteristics as a whole, a theological method can be deduced which has been indicative of Orthodox theologizing through the centuries. It is called an apophatic (or negative) method of theologizing in the East, contrasted to the cataphatic (or affirmative) theologizing practiced in the Latin West. Admittedly, all theological knowledge is based upon revelation. "The East, in its longing for union with God, sees this revelation as a foretaste of the world to come (the vision), the reflection of a light through a cloud of unknowing, a seeing which causes us to desire a still greater brightness, a subdued light rather than a shining brilliance."[46] The Christian West on the other hand, from its viewpoint, "is more conscious of the positive aspect of this Revelation, of all that it adds to the knowledge which we can acquire by natural reason in its own right. It thus sees more the luminous aspect of dogma, for it is by this dogma that God speaks to us and desires to give us a definite direction by which we, and through us the world, may be guided on our way towards himself. For the West, Revelation is a light, *lumen vitae;* a substitute to doubt, in many ways gravely imperfect, but none the less a God-given substitute for the light of the beatific vision, and which thus possesses the intellectual precision of a canon or rule: *'regula fidei.'* "[47] The same revelation is then seen from two points of view—the East views theology as a way of mystic union, and the West sees theology as a way of defining the pilgrim's course of action on earth.

According to Orthodox theologian Vladimir Lossky, the cataphatic "leads us to some knowledge of God, but it is an imperfect way. The perfect way, the only way which is fitting in regard to God, who is of His very nature unknowable,"[48] is the apophatic, "which leads us finally to total ignorance. All knowledge has as its object that which is. Now God is beyond all that exists. In order to approach Him it is necessary to deny all that is inferior to Him, that is to say, all that which is. If in seeing God one can know what one sees, then one has not seen God in Himself but something intelligible, something which is inferior to Him. It is by *unknowing* (*agnōsia*) that one may know Him who is above every possible object of knowledge. Proceeding by negations one ascends from the inferior degrees of being to the highest, by progressively setting aside all that can be known, in order to draw near to the Unknown in the darkness of absolute ignorance. For even as light, and especially abundance of light, renders darkness invisible; even so the knowledge of created things, and especially excess of knowledge, destroys the ignorance which is the only way by which one can attain to God in Himself."[49] To illustrate this way of theologizing, note how John of Damascus expresses himself in his *Exposition of the Orthodox Faith* (*De fide orthodoxa*):

God then is infinite and incomprehensible: and all that is comprehensible about Him is His infinity and incomprehensibility. But all that we can affirm concerning God does not shew forth God's nature, but only the qualities of His nature. For when you speak of Him as good, and just, and wise, and so forth, you do not tell God's nature but only the qualities of His nature. Further there are some affirmations which we make concerning God which have the force of absolute negation: for example, when we use the term darkness, in reference to God, we do not mean darkness itself, but that He is not light but above light: and when we speak of Him as light, we mean that His is not darkness.[50]

Orthodox theologizing does not believe in "systematic theologies" as such, for the undercurrent in her whole process of thinking is one of "holy agnosticism."[51] Her theology is pneumatically oriented, whereas the theology of the West is a theology of the Word that seeks to speak to the rationality of man. Eastern theology desires to go beyond man's rationality, reflecting upon the divine mysteries "diffused as it were through a dark cloud. In its desire to be united with the source of this reflection, it is always striving to rise above the reflection, partial and limited as it inevitably is, towards the infinite flame itself. Apophatic theology is precisely this constant ever-upward movement of desire, which despises all earthly or merely human limitations."[52]

In the West, revelation is like the sky with its stars giving light to the night. "It attaches itself to their light, feeble though it is, and seeks to capture it as it converges in order to illuminate the road, as the course of a ship is regulated by the stars, hence its preoccupation to remain on the level of a rational method which progresses only from one ray of light to the next, avoiding such an excess of light that the result is only a higher kind of darkness. Such is the way of affirmative theology, which follows the method of human discourse, moving carefully on from one point to the next in order to arrive at the conclusion. It is this difference of conception which explains the diversity of theological method."[53] The West places confidence upon human reason to translate the meaning of the revelation, whereas the East rejects human reason as a limited vehicle and views the revelational data simply as a porthole through which we *sense* the mystery and wonder of what is beyond the horizon.

To sum up, the revelation of the one faith is differently received and developed by the East and the West. Apophatic theology of the East prefers the method of negation and paradox (antinomy) as a way of reaching for divine reality which is beyond all concepts and all discourse. "If God essentially surpasses the capacities of the human mind, it is argued, it can only be possible to attain Him in the realm which lies beyond understanding, by transcending the methods which are proper to ordinary knowledge in simultaneous affirmation and negation. God 'is'; God 'is' not—these two affirmations are both equally true and equally untrue."[54] Cataphatic or affirmative theology "is quite different from this, for it seizes hold of the positive content of the affirmations of the faith. It has confidence in the power of reason as it seeks to confront them with the aid of the principle of analogy, yet at the same time it is careful to understand these affirmations aright and to guard against premature conclusions or syntheses."[55]

An ecumenical spirit of theologizing for the future will need to extend itself beyond this contrast as practiced in the East and West if there is to be more meaningful dialogue among Christians for the sake of the one tradition, once revealed to all the saints. It is therefore incumbent upon Protestants as well as Orthodox to follow the *living* spirit and common heritage of the church fathers as we continue for our day the responsible task of theologizing, caught as were our forefathers in the never-ending tension between the needs for assurance and the knowledge that all which we think we "know" remains subject to his Spirit. Nevertheless, we are hurled forward by the dynamics of his unsystematized Spirit, whose power transcends our traditions and whose presence both humbles and inspires us as it did our forefathers in the faith.

Chapter III

Missions, Proselytism, and the Future

Orthodoxy is actually as missionary-minded as Protestantism and Roman Catholicism. This statement will surprise the majority of Protestants and Roman Catholics. It has long been assumed and accepted that Orthodox churches are nationalist churches and therefore lack the missionary concern necessary for them to break out from these self-imposed boundaries.[1] Archbishop Iakovos, head of the Greek Orthodox Archdiocese of North and South America, and one of the presidents of the World Council of Churches, presided over that now historic session of the Third Assembly of the World Council of Churches at New Delhi which saw the Council's integration with the International Missionary Council. His presence at this session was a symbolic and significant indication that Orthodoxy is taking seriously its missionary responsibility in the body of Christ.

Signs of Vitality

There are some noteworthy signs of renewal and vitality regarding missionary concern within Orthodoxy which can be examined. First and foremost is the establishment, in 1961, of an Inter-Orthodox Missionary Center under the name Porefthendes, in Athens. The purpose of this Center is to promote within Orthodoxy the aims of missionary outreach, education, financial support, and the enlistment of personnel. The general director of the Center is Father Anastasios Yannoulatos and the scope of its work is: (1) study and research on the theoretical and practical problems of Orthodox external mission; (2) the fostering of a missionary and ecumenical conscience within the Orthodox Church throughout the world; (3) assistance for the spiritual and scientific education of prospective missionaries; (4) contact with the missionary churches and help in solving theoretical and organizational problems which arise.[2] The healthy spirit manifested in the founding of this Center cannot be denied.

It is interesting to note that the inspiration behind the Center's creation has come from the youth of Orthodoxy, with the full blessing of the Ecumenical Patriarch Athenagoras. By youth I mean the international organization of Orthodox youth movements known as Syndesmos.[3] This organization, founded in Paris in April, 1953, is an assembly of Orthodox youth of different national churches. Its Greek name, Syndesmos, means "bond" or "link," taken from Eph. 4:3, "Eager to maintain the unity of the Spirit in the bond (*syndesmos*) of peace." The fifth General Assembly of Syndesmos met in the summer of 1961 in Beirut, Lebanon, on the theme "Church and Mission," and out of this conference came the establishment of the Inter-Orthodox Missionary Center.

In addition to the Center, signs of vitality may be seen in the initiation of an Institute of Afro-Asian Studies in Thessalonica. This institute, which is affiliated with the theological school of the University of Thessalonica, is designed to meet the needs of Orthodox students from Asia and Africa in various fields.[4] Not long ago, the first African Orthodox priest was ordained. The priest, Father Theodoros Nankyamas,[5] is to assist in the growing community in Uganda. The African Orthodox Church today consists of fifty-six communities, numbering some twenty thousand Africans in Kenya, Tanganyika, and Uganda. One reason behind the increasing number of African Orthodox Christians in recent years is an appeal free of the weight of nineteenth-century colonial stigma so often associated with Roman Catholicism and Protestantism.[6]

Also in 1961, four young students of St. Vladimir's Orthodox
Theological Seminary in New York gave themselves to the
Orthodox Mission in Alaska. In Athens, a young Korean is
studying for the priesthood, hoping to return for missionary
activity in his homeland, where a small Orthodox community
now exists in Seoul. The most significant fact to observe is that
the youth of Orthodoxy recognize that missionary responsibility
crosses national boundaries which their fathers formerly accepted as delimiting; this is one of the surest signs of revival
today. As Father Yannoulatos expresses it:

We do not preserve Orthodoxy simply by admiring her life
of worship and her doctrine. The consciousness of the fact that
"God hath made all men of one blood" (Acts 17:26) and that
"He wants all men to be saved and come to the knowledge of
truth" (I Tim. 2:4) forms an inseparable element of Orthodoxy.
The salvation of "all the world" is a doctrine of the Church.
And we must accept the consequences. A Church which shows
no missionary activity, which does not participate in Christ's
agony on the Cross for the salvation of the entire world, for the
growth of the Body of the Church into its final dimensions, for
the accomplishment of the divine plan of Redemption (see
Matt., ch. 24), is not really an alive Body of Christ, truly Orthodox, a guard of the spirit of the "one holy, catholic and
apostolic Church" to which our Lord entrusted the continua-
tion of His redemptive work.[7]

Historic Orthodox Missionary Activity

It should not be forgotten, as we observe the present signs of
renewal and vitality, that Eastern Orthodoxy has a rich heritage of missionary activity. We cannot go into great detail
here, but we can indicate some of the missionary highlights of
the past.[8] Looking back to the seventh century, we are reminded of the early and wide missionary accomplishments of
the Nestorians who proclaimed the gospel throughout Central
Asia.[9] Later, in the ninth century, the Byzantine Church with

its base in Constantinople sent out two brothers from Thessalonica as apostles to the Slavic people—the Serbs, the Bulgarians and those in Russia. Their names, Cyril and Methodius, are canonized today as "equals to the Apostles." Their approach was to master the language and then proceed to translate the Christian Byzantine liturgy into the Slavic dialects. The method used by these two Greek brothers was met with opposition by the Frankish missionaries of the West.

For example, the introduction of a Slavonic liturgy into Moravia was attacked harshly by the Frankish missionaries. According to Byzantine sources, the Greek missionaries were accused of a new heresy, the "heresy of the three languages,"[10] which maintained that only three languages were worthy to express the Word of God, namely, Hebrew, Greek, and Latin. "The Byzantines had no difficulty in refuting this curious theory, and the Greek Church triumphed everywhere that political circumstances allowed. Thus the majority of the Slavs embraced Orthodoxy, adopted the Cyrillic alphabet (named after Cyril), and were integrated into the Byzantine ecclesiastical world."[11] Finally, with the baptism of Prince Vladimir at the end of the tenth century, Russia joined the family of Christian nations and was, until 1917, the chief initiator of modern Orthodox missions.

During the period 1237 to 1480 the Russians sent priests and monks out to the Mongol, Lithuanian, and Finnish tribes. In 1658, Russia founded her missions in China and among the Muslims, and later, in 1794, her first mission in Alaska. In the 1860's she began missions in Japan, Korea, and Manchuria, and in 1882 established work in the Near and Middle East among the Arabic-speaking Syrians. Also, during this time the first Orthodox church in South America was begun. The Orthodox Missionary Society was founded in Moscow on January 25, 1870.[12]

The main reason for Russian leadership in missionary activity is the fact that the Orthodox churches of the Near East and of the Balkan peninsula were deprived by the Turks, right up to the beginning of the twentieth century, of any possibility of expansion. This allowed only the Orthodox Church of Russia, unfettered by foreign domination, the freedom of action to carry out a mission program.[13]

There have been many outstanding Orthodox leaders behind the mission activities of the Russian Church. We can mention only a few. St. Stephen of Perm (1340–1396), one of the first missionaries of the Russian Church, like Cyril and Methodius, proceeded to translate the gospel into the language of the Zyrians, a savage population of the northern forests. This was followed by the building of a church and a school. St. Stephen's example later inspired other priests and laymen to translate the Scriptures and liturgy into many other languages found throughout the expanse of Russia, such as the Votyak, Nogai, Cheremis, Tartar, Chuvash, Yakut, Tungusic, Buryat, Aleutian, Kolosh, Karelian, Samoyed, and others—and not to be forgotten are the Far Eastern languages, Chinese, Japanese, and Korean.[14]

St. Tryphon (1495–1583) illustrates the role of laymen in missionary work. Later becoming a monk but never losing his lay status, he carried the gospel to the Lapps and founded Pechenga, the most northerly of Russian monasteries. Other laymen, such as Cyril Soukhanov, who went to the Unguz nomads, and Paul Afansiev, who went to the North Koreans, preached and taught with very meager financial resources.[15]

Nikita Struve, editor of *Le Messager Orthodoxe*, reports that "from the sixteenth century until the end of the eighteenth, missionary expansion was more closely linked with the fortunes of the state which gradually succeeded in imposing its tutelage upon the Church."[16] In 1555, Czar Ivan the Terrible commissioned Bishop Gurji to preach the gospel among the Muslims in Russia at Kazan. The results of his missionary activity were surprising when compared with Protestant and Roman Catholic encounters with Islam.[17] Thousands of Muslims were converted to Christianity. Bishop Gurji built a monastery and missionary training school, and the latter half of the nineteenth century was to see the establishment of the Ecclesiastical Academy of Kazan.[18] Later, Peter the Great sent Philotheus Lestchinski (1650–1727), Bishop of Tobolsk, into Siberia. Many thousands of natives in the area were converted through his evangelical zeal. In 1714, Peter the Great commanded the first Orthodox mission in China, but in this case, as in others, the outward support of the state also carried diplomatic involvement which hindered rather than helped the cause of the missionaries. In short, it cannot be denied that state support was responsible for Orthodox missionary activity, but there are numerous cases in which the opposite was true and barriers were placed in the paths of the missionaries.[19]

In the nineteenth century, missionary endeavors by the Russians experienced a marked revival under the leadership of Macarius Glukharev (1792–1847), John Veniaminov (1797–1879), and Nicholas Kassatkin (1836–1912). Glukharev is noted as the apostle to the Altai people in the region of Siberia and was the first to develop an embryonic missionary theology that was later developed and refined by Nikolay Ilminski. Veniaminov is referred to as the apostle of Alaska and of the Siberian East. He became the first bishop of North America and later, due to his outstanding mission work, Metropolitan of Moscow. He was responsible for establishing the Orthodox Missionary Society and for setting aside the Sunday of Orthodoxy (the first Sunday in Lent) for collections to support the widespread missionary efforts of Orthodoxy. Kassatkin, known as the apostle of Japan, went first to this island kingdom as chaplain to the Russian Consulate and in a short time found himself concerned for the spiritual welfare of the Japanese. At this period, Christianity was still a forbidden religion in Japan. "Father Nicholas succeeded none the less in converting a Shintoist priest, Swabe, an implacable enemy of foreigners, Sakai, a doctor, and a third Japanese. With the help of these three he

set to work immediately on the translation of the Scriptures and
of the liturgical books. In 1871, Father Nicholas, whose community now numbered twelve baptized Christians and twenty-
five catechumens, returned to Russia and persuaded the Holy
Synod to organize officially an Orthodox mission. Two years
later Father Nicholas was laying the first foundations in Tokyo
of the Orthodox Cathedral of the Resurrection, which was to
become (and still is) the most beautiful Christian building in
Japan, was inaugurating a seminary for the training of an indigenous clergy and a school for catechists, and was entrusting
a committee of nine members with the translation of works on
Orthodoxy into Japanese."[20]

Suffice it to say that after the Russian Revolution the freedom
to promote missions was curtailed, but the work that was begun
in various countries continues to exist and to thrive, with indigenous leadership, often in difficult circumstances, as in the
Peoples Republic of China, Japan, Korea, and elsewhere. Re-
liable statistics are not available, but we suspect that these
small communities of Orthodox Christians are often making
their Christian witness very effectively because of their affinity
to Asian culture.

Much of the success of the Russian Church's missionary activity was clearly inspired by the principles laid down by the
illustrious Russian Orientalist, Nikolay Ilminski (1822–1891):
(1) Orthodoxy must be preached to each nation in its own
tongue. This meant that each mission must translate the sacred
Scriptures and Orthodox liturgical books into the language of
the people. (2) As soon as possible, indigenous clergy and
teachers must be trained and the Russians withdrawn. (3) Each
mission should be made ready to stand on its own feet without
continuing to rely on Russian funds and missionaries. The
church would thus avoid bureaucracy and be prevented from
making the mission churches into imitations of Russian
churches.[21] It is surprising how modern these principles sound
to our ears, especially when we are reminded that they come
from an Orthodox Christian of the nineteenth century.[22]

Forecast for the Future

In the light of both the current signs of vitality and the past history of Orthodox missions, there are several positive implications that can be seen as well as several potentially negative ones that must be honestly confessed, and by the grace of God avoided. Positively, we are heartened by the fact that nationalist boundaries are being broken in Orthodoxy, thereby reestablishing the missionary imperative which is inherent in true Orthodoxy.[23] Furthermore, the present missionary reawakening has the approval of the church's hierarchy, but significantly the weight of responsibility is being carried by the youth, which ensures a promising future. Also, we should note that the clergy and laity of the church are together supporting the revival, and in Orthodoxy this is never a factor to be taken lightly, since the theologically trained laity are often less conservative than the clergy in pursuing new ideas. Finally, Orthodox churchmen are beginning to see that fellow Christians in the member churches of the World Council of Churches can indicate many instructive and helpful techniques from their experiences in carrying out missionary progress. For example, during the summer of 1961 the writer saw such simple and meaningful sharing at the Ecumenical Institute at Bossey, Switzerland, during a course for pastors and missionaries. There a Greek Orthodox churchman "cornered" an experienced Lutheran missionary who had spent the greater part of his life laboring among the Papuans of New Guinea. He asked him countless questions, eagerly making notes to report to his group. Later he remarked to me, "That is exactly the kind of work which my church wants to do too."

There are, however, implications in this new fraternization which must be seen as potentially negative, and be overcome. A conscious mistrust remains that relations between Protestant and Orthodox Christians (and Roman Catholics too) may lead eventually to *proselytizing* (perhaps in more subtle forms than in the past) rather than to effective witnessing before non-

Christians. Proselytizing, of course, violates the integrity of all Christian traditions. Western missionaries have been accused of proselytizing among Eastern Christians in the past, especially where Islam has held sway,[24] even as today Western Christians are accusing Eastern Christians of proselytism in reference to the Orthodox mission in Africa.[25] There is a sense in which all the respective Christian traditions, motivated with enthusiasm both for the gospel and for their churches, have at times confused witnessing with proselytizing. "Proselytism is not something absolutely different from witness; it is the corruption of witness. When cajolery, bribery, undue pressures of intimidation are used—subtly or openly—to bring about seeming conversion; when we put the success of our church before the honor of Christ; when we commit the dishonesty of comparing the ideal of our own church with the actual achievement of another; when we seek to advance our own cause by bearing false witness against another church; when personal or corporate self-seeking replaces love for every individual soul with whom we are concerned—then witness has been deformed into proselytism. It is very easy for us to recognize these sins in others; it is necessary to acknowledge that we are all liable to fall into one or another of them ourselves."[26] We can readily see that there is a real distinction between witness and proselytism in purpose, motive, and spirit—the means and ends of each are antithetical to the other.

However, it is not enough to distinguish witnessing from proselytism. We must go on to answer the other question of how we can have freedom in our Christian witnessing within the widening ecumenical atmosphere that exists among Christians today. Churches of all traditions have been hurt in the past, and as a result our present ecumenical ties are suspected and strained in some quarters. Today, for example, one has only to travel in Orthodox lands to experience the hostility and resentment toward Protestant missions. The real issue is not whether the resentment is justified or not (for, frankly, in some cases it is not), but rather the heart of the matter is that this

hostility has undermined and limited the growth of our ecumenical relations with one another. Ecumenicity cannot be fos-
tered where there is mistrust and lack of confidence in one another's intentions. There is an unfinished task of mission ahead
for all Christians, and nothing less than a concerted effort
toward reconciliation among the churches is necessary if we
are to realize our goal.

In today's ecumenical era we must each learn to confess the
shortcomings of the past, accepting the fact of the young
churches that now exist as expressions of God's judgment and
God's grace which came about in spite of ourselves. Together
we must look ahead for creative new beginnings, urged on by the
Holy Spirit to go beyond narrow-minded confessional polemics,
and address ourselves anew to the unending task of mission.

Concretely, potential negativism can be overcome by increasing the contact between Christians of the East and those
of the West, not so much on earlier battlefields where past hostility is not entirely gone, but rather by concentrating on one
another's "backyards." That is to say, greater opportunities
should be found for the exchange of theological students—for
example, by Protestants studying in Orthodox lands, as well as
by an increase in the number of Orthodox students in Protestant
schools. The exchange of students, books, scholars, and techniques must all be developed and continued until we are able
to speak one another's "spiritual language," learning to listen
together to the one Spirit of God calling us to go out and proclaim the good news of the gospel. To this end, it would be
both exciting and stimulating to see a permanent East-West
institute where this exchange of ideas, aims, and personnel
might take place. Thus as a result of the enrichment gained
through mutual contacts—East with West—together we shall
be able to enter into the deeper mysteries and glories of the
Triune God who has called us to fulfill his great commission. In
this respect, the scope of Orthodoxy's vital concern for mission
—past, present and future—can be nothing less than a source
of greatest joy for all Christians of goodwill.

Part Two

DIMENSIONS OF THE CHURCH

Chapter IV

Eastern Catholicity

Conversations on "catholicity" and "collegiality" are currently receiving wide and extensive coverage in ecumenical circles both in the East and in the West.[1] The two related topics received much attention at the Second Vatican Council. The concept of collegiality approved by the Council Fathers seeks to further the reality of catholicity in the Roman Church. In essence the idea of collegiality declares that bishops, as descendants of the apostles, share ruling authority over the church with the pope. The implications of this shared authority have yet to be realized, as evidenced in the third session where the pope, and not the bishops, wielded ultimate power at the session's adjournment. Disappointment and disillusionment were expressed by Roman and non-Roman churchmen, as they hopefully look for further clarification and reassessment of the situation in these post-Vatican II years.

In the meantime, Eastern Orthodox and Protestant Christians within the structure of the World Council of Churches (Faith and Order Commission) have also been raising the question of catholicity in discussing the ecclesiological significance of the councils of churches.[2] Many Christians outside the Roman Catholic communion were (and still are) hopeful that the idea of collegiality will serve as a potential bridge to extend the discussion on catholicity beyond the present respective boundaries, encouraging the eventual embrace of the whole of Christendom.

In particular, some Roman Catholics and Eastern churchmen anticipated a possible awakening from centuries of separation through a rightful understanding of collegiality. It was
hoped by many that collegiality would favorably complement
the Eastern concept of catholicity.[3] Does the West, however,
sufficiently appreciate Eastern ecclesiology? Is collegiality,
from an Eastern viewpoint, but another premature attempt at
reconciliation by the West?[4] Before these questions can be answered, we must clearly understand the Orthodox concept of
catholicity.

Catholicity as *Sobornost'*

Orthodox catholicity has been commonly defined in terms of
sobornost', which is taken from its use in the Slavonic text of
the Nicene Creed and is used interchangeably with the word
"catholic." Etymologically, the word *sobornost'* is derived from
the root *sobirat,* meaning "to reunite," "to assemble." *Sobirat* in
turn comes from *sobor,* which conveys the dual meaning of
"council" and "church." *Sobornost',* in short, implies the state of
being together, and in relation to the church points to a *conciliar* assembly of churchmen gathered together in a spirit of
love and freedom. The concept of *sobornost'* symbolizes the
harmony and unanimity that should represent the primary
characteristic of the church's catholicity. Orthodox catholicity
seeks this spirit of harmonious unanimity, which in practice is
conciliar, creatively synthesizing the individuality of its members into a unified authority of the One, Holy, Catholic, and
Apostolic Church.[5]

A succinct and well-formed expression of Orthodox catholicity for our day was written by the celebrated Alexis Khomiakov, a lay Russian Orthodox theologian, through his essay *The
Church Is One,* first published in 1864. He emphasized that the
catholicity of the church means not only universality and ubi-
quity, but above all, *unity.* The unity of the church resides in
the triune unity of the Godhead. Khomiakov wrote:

The church is one. Her unity follows of necessity from the unity of God; for the Church is not a multitude of persons in their separate individuality, but a unity of the grace of God, living in a multitude of rational creatures, submitting themselves willingly to grace. Grace, indeed, is also given to those who resist it, and to those who do not make use of it (who hide their talent in the earth), but these are not in the Church. In fact, the unity of the Church is not imaginary or allegorical, but a true and substantial unity, such as is the unity of many members in a living body.

The Church is one, notwithstanding her division as it appears to a man who is still alive on earth. It is only in relation to man that it is possible to recognize a division of the Church into visible and invisible; her unity is, in reality, true and absolute. Those who are alive on earth, those who have finished their earthly course, those who, like the angels, were not created for a life on earth, those in future generations who have not yet begun their earthly course, are all united together in one Church, in one and the same grace of God; for the creation of God which has not yet been manifested is manifest to Him; and God hears the prayers and knows the faith of those whom He has not yet called out of non-existence into existence. Indeed the Church, the Body of Christ, is manifesting forth and fulfilling herself in time, without changing her essential unity or inward life of grace. And therefore, when we speak of "the Church visible and invisible," we so speak only in relation to man.[6]

This unified view of catholicity expressed by Khomiakov is sustained and governed by the work and person of the Holy Spirit. Fragmentation and multiplicity in the church, which tend so often to cause disunity and destroy catholicity, are spared by the Orthodox insistence upon the sovereignty of the Spirit within the life of the church. Hence, Orthodoxy is able to maintain her unity in spite of the divergent autocephality within her ranks.[7] The multiplicity stemming from autocephality is an opportunity for Orthodoxy to express oneness of spirit and of thought while simultaneously advocating diversity

within her fellowship. Obviously, there is a dynamic quality inherent in her catholicity which is far more significant than any
quantitative standards of catholicity found in the West, where
external numerical strength and structural cohesion are measured. The Orthodox standard of catholicity is qualitative, encompassing freedom and fulfillment for the individual believer
who shares a oneness of spirit with his fellow believers, an inward rather than an outward unity.

Likewise, *ecumenicity for Orthodoxy is qualitative rather
than quantitative*. From this perspective, true ecumenicity for
Orthodoxy is synonymous with true catholicity.[8] Since Orthodoxy avoids uniformity in her quest for oneness, her sense of
unity is not forced upon the believer or upon any particular
autocephalous church. The tension and necessary balance
among the contrasting members is maintained by the Holy
Spirit.

Furthermore, it is the indwelling of the Holy Spirit in the
church which in turn makes the church infallible and holy.
"None is holy but the Universal Church itself. Consequently,
only the Church is infallible. Infallibility and holiness are inseparable. No particular Church and no bishop may presume
to dictate the faith to the whole Church without sinking into
pride and falling away. The right understanding of religious
truth is given only to those who live a holy life. This understanding does not belong to an office, as is taught in the Roman
Church, nor to correct scholarship, as is often implied in Protestantism."[9] To state the matter positively, the Lord of the
Church—namely, the Holy Spirit—in Orthodox theology, sets
forth the characteristics of catholicity, which are: a conciliatory
spirit of unity and mutuality, a qualitative ecumenicity, holiness, and historic continuity which stems from the Nicene-Constantinopolitan Creed and the definitions of the early ecumenical councils which sought to remain faithful to the apostolic
tradition. The combination of all these characteristics expresses
the meaning and significance of *sobornost'*, a grand synthesis of
authority and individuality in love which unites all believers.

Catholicity, or *sobornost'* for Orthodoxy, belongs, then, to the church as a whole under the Holy Spirit.

Sobornost' or the Papacy?

With the concept of *sobornost'* clearly in focus, we can begin to anticipate Orthodoxy's historic resistance to the Roman Church and the concept of catholicity demonstrated in the papacy. Has the new Roman emphasis of collegiality narrowed the separation from Constantinople? Is it the intention of the Latin Church to strive for internal catholicity—that is, for qualitative ecumenicity as deemed necessary by the Greek Church? "While the new emphasis on 'collegiality' is clearly a positive one, does it exhaust," asks Orthodox theologian John Meyendorff, "the traditional Church's teaching on episcopacy? This teaching proclaims that a bishop is a member of the universal episcopate, not *ex sese,* but in virtue of his being the sacramental head of a diocese, of which he has been consecrated a bishop. The traditional and weightiest Orthodox objection against Roman ecclesiology has always been that 'apostolicity' and 'episcopacy' cannot be simply identified, although the latter proceeds from the former and, through 'apostolic succession,' shares in some of its functions."[10] According to Orthodox ecclesiology, the position of the local church, including its priest and laity, not only that of bishops, is essential and needs to be recognized. This recognition is provided by *sobornost',* which consciously aims for a *unity of persons* who make up the body of Christ. It seems, practically speaking, that this integral unified concept of episcopacy leading to internal catholicity is absent in the present thinking of the Second Vatican Council. "For the 'collegiality' of bishops is not the power of a self-perpetuating body of individuals *over* the Church; it is the witness, sanctioned by the Holy Spirit and by Apostolic succession, of the universal agreement of all local churches in the true faith. St. Cyprian of Carthage used to say about each local community: 'The bishop is in the Church, and the Church is in the

bishop.' "[11] Collegiality as interpreted by the Roman Church
does not yet reach the scope and depth sought by Orthodoxy.

The Orthodox believe at this point that the Roman Church
does not intend to break from the 1870 definition of Vatican I
on the episcopal jurisdiction of the pope over all the faithful.
How, then, can collegiality, in itself a sound principle, have
any real effect unless the 1870 definition is drastically rede-
fined? It seems to the Orthodox "that no *real* progress will be
made towards unity, and the present impression of a vicious
circle, created by the definition of Vatican I, will remain, as
long as the structural definitions of the Roman Church continue to stress the dependence of the bishops upon the Pope
without admitting any real dependence of the Pope upon the
entire body of the Church. Rome does not seem ready for a
definition implying such an *interdependence,* although it
slowly moves in that direction."[12] Hence, we can begin to appreciate Orthodox theologian Nissiotis' reaction to Vatican II
when he raises the question, "Is the Vatican Council really ecumenical?"[13] Is it the intention of the Council, while admittedly
Pan-Roman, to understand catholicity as *sobornost'* rather than
in terms of the papacy? Catholicity as *sobornost'* is the only true
dimension of ecumenicity acceptable to Orthodox theology,
and it is indeed questionable whether this can be seen in the
present Vatican Council. The symbol and power of the Petrine
Office "has in Orthodox eyes falsified the whole concept of ecclesiology and practical discipline so that the *Ecclesia* is defined in universalistic, geographic and quantitative terms only,
neglecting its other meaning, the ancient qualitative meaning
based on the eucharistic gathering with the local bishop in
every place, creating new autocephalous local churches without subordinating them to one juridical centre."[14] Actually, the
present premature concept of collegiality has the grave danger
of widening rather than healing the gap between the separated
churches and especially between the Roman Church and Orthodoxy.[15]

The Orthodox readily admit that the *schemata de ecclesia*

demonstrates an earnest effort of Rome "to speak positively about the ministry of the bishops, but on the basis of a rather weak exegesis of Matt. 16:18. The distinction is drawn between Peter as the first of the Apostles and the Eleven, and an analogy is made to put forward the two lines which proceed from Christ and the call of the Twelve. The one: Christ—Peter— Pope; and the other: Christ—the Eleven—bishops. Alongside this call of the Twelve by Jesus there is no mention of the event of Pentecost and its implication for the whole episcopacy as rooted in the community of the faithful, creating the presupposition for a right understanding of the equality of the bishops without exception, as bishops at the same time of local churches and of the whole *Ecclesia*."[16] Nevertheless, the present Roman interpretation of collegiality for the Orthodox is both non-Biblical and nonhistoric, and does not really begin to grapple with the dynamics of internal catholicity viewed as *sobornost'*.

From another perspective, it must be said that Roman Catholics are well aware that the position and power of the papacy as it now stands is a problem for the Orthodox. Most Roman theologians and apologists in this regard have insisted that the difference is not as great as it first appears. Roman Catholics wish to stress that they too have *sobornost'*, but approach the problem in a way different from that of the East. Catholic theologians emphasize that "the Roman Pontiff is bishop of a local diocese like his brothers in the episcopate, but in addition Christ has entrusted to him a special office: to guard, in his capacity as successor of Peter on the see of Rome, the unity of the Sobornost' itself."[17] The Catholics want it to be noted that "in affirming the universality in extent and depth of the pontifical jurisdiction is the best guarantee of the world-wide significance, that is to say of the Catholicity, of the power which he is recognized as possessing: he is not the 'greatest among his brethren,' he is the 'representative' or symbol of the Sobornost', the living incarnation of the solidarity of the bishops. . . . This is surely, in other words, to say that in the exercise of his power he must without ceasing have regard for the

true structure of the Church, governed as it is by a college of
bishops; and always act with the *common* good in view, conscious of being himself the organ and support of the hierarchy."[18] The Orthodox, however, do not understand how catholicity as *sobornost'* can be personified in the papacy rather
than in the total membership of the church.

Although Roman theologians attempt to adjust to the qualitative sense of unity expressed by *sobornost'*, they essentially
do not shift from a *pyramid ecclesiology* which starts from the
top down rather than from the base of the pyramid; in contrast,
the Orthodox start with the base, beginning with the chief cornerstone, namely, Jesus Christ, followed by the apostles, the
faithful (clergy and laity including the elected bishops), until
finally the apex is reached and symbolized as a place of honor
in the office of the Ecumenical Patriarch and/or the Pope.
(The Orthodox are willing to grant to the latter the primacy of
honor.) Unless the base of the pyramid is given priority, the
Orthodox believe, the entire *charismatic* life of the whole
church will be relegated to a secondary position of importance.
The result will be the entire loss of an *internal and inclusive
catholicity* which alone can experience the depth and wonder
of oneness built upon the chief cornerstone of the church, Jesus
Christ.

Orthodoxy and Protestant Catholicity

Protestants can certainly appreciate the dynamic, interper-
sonal quality of catholicity advocated by Orthodoxy. For Prot-
testants, too, catholicity begins with a confession of Jesus
Christ as the chief cornerstone of the church. Catholicity is the
task "of allowing the fulness of Christ to be manifest in the
Church. As an image through which the Church understands
what it is to be the Church, catholicity is thus always a call for
expression and practice rather than a quality to be claimed as
a possession. Every effort to articulate the meaning of cath-

olicity must be read as reference to the wholeness in Christ and toward which the Church must grow."[19] Hence, the present involvement and commitment of Protestantism (unfortunately not all Protestants) in the ecumenical movement, and specifically in dialogue with Orthodoxy on an intensified level, are not for the sake of superficial compromises and alignments, but far more to seek a unity in terms of mutual enrichment, exchanges in freedom and love, realizing that ultimate oneness is an unmerited gift from the Lord of the church himself. Ecumenicity for Protestants, as for Orthodox, is a common striving for obedience to Christ. It does not imply uniformity, since this did not exist among the Twelve. Ecumenicity, like catholicity, is an expression of unity in Christ and not institutional uniformity. Its aim is a mutual sharing around a common center, a community of humanity dominated by the presence of Christ in the Holy Spirit. Catholicity for Protestants points toward a *koinōnia* of churches, which in mutual love and respect will have fellowship with one another, break bread and drink together. Protestant ecumenicity, with its goal of catholicity, must not settle for less than an integral Eucharistic celebration of the Word.

Of course, for Protestants there are weighty differences with Orthodoxy as well as with Roman Catholicism which would take us beyond our present limits of study. However, it is sufficient to note here that Orthodox must come to realize that Protestants are as concerned with the subject of catholicity as they are. In many ways, Protestants need to consider Orthodox as elder brothers in the faith, especially in the latter's relation to Rome. Much of our current disenchantment with Vatican II is caused by our relatively short history of dialogue with Rome and her workings as compared to that of Eastern Christendom. Protestants could well take some pointers from Orthodoxy in understanding Rome. In the meantime, Orthodoxy must come to look upon Protestantism as more than simply a phenomenon of disruptive individualism. Calvin and Luther were opposed to anarchic individualism as manifested by some Protestant ex-

tremists. Both Orthodoxy and Protestantism reacted to autocratic papal rule in order to maintain the internal integrity of
catholicity.

Positively, Orthodoxy and Protestantism are advocating an
ordered liberty in the church's common life and throughout the
oikoumenē. There is in both traditions the synodical or conciliar idea expressed by *sobornost'*.[20] While the hierarchical
form of government in Orthodoxy differs from that of most of
Protestantism, the external organizations of the two traditions
are to a remarkable degree similar. For example, neither has a
monolithic structure. Orthodoxy consists of several autocephalous churches, each of them independent from the others, but
all of them in communion with each other. Protestant denom-
inations, while independent of one another, are increasing the
practice of intercommunion and other activities with one another.

In spite of the above areas of similarity, the fact looms large
that the Western roots of Protestantism as opposed to the Eastern roots of Orthodoxy have resulted in contrasting theological
methodology, worship, sacraments, and other doctrinal matters
pertaining to the life of the church, which will stimuate healthy
conversations for many years to come. The important aspect to
underline is that in these varying approaches we are able to
speak as partners in dialogue who are sincerely desirous of realizing the catholicity of the body of Christ, knowing that the
World Council and Vatican II are at best but instruments to
that end.

In conclusion, this chapter would be incomplete without
mentioning that future discussions must extend beyond individual traditions, whether Catholicism, Orthodoxy, or Protestantism. Tomorrow's theologians and churchmen will need to
emphasize, as did the apostles, that the mission of Christ and
his church is indivisible. In Christ there is truly no East or
West, but one, holy, catholic, and apostolic *koinōnia* of churches,
living under the one cross of Christ.[21]

Chapter V

The Visible and Invisible Church

The world confessional gatherings of Protestants, Orthodox, or Roman Catholics, such as those held at Helsinki, Frankfurt, Rhodes, Addis Ababa, and the Vatican, have discussed and will continue to discuss at future consultations their respective theological understandings of issues from the standpoint of their ecclesiology. Close to the center of each of their views of the church lies the concept of the visible and invisible church. This concept serves as a basic point of reference in the framework of all their discussions and deliberations. Certainly, in this ecumenical era, it is both very relevant and necessary to look once again at the familiar but ambiguous distinction between the visible and invisible church. What are we to make of it? The distinction itself carries both truths and obstacles in all interconfessional conversations.

Traditionally interpreted, the visible church points to the institutional church in the world, whereas the invisible church consists of the totality of all true believers irrespective of their affiliations or lack of them with any organizationally constituted church.[1] The question can immediately be raised whether the reality of the church before us (*ecclesia militans*) has any such polarity of distinction as visible and invisible. What is the original intention behind this kind of distinction? Is it justified in continuing to exist or has such a concept been of greater harm than use in our understanding of the church? All these questions may be rightly raised, for it has been not only Protestants, but also Orthodox and Roman Catholics who have been troubled in determining who is and who isn't a member of the visible household of God, and therefore consciously and even unconsciously have been pressed to work out the implications inherent in the distinction between the visible and invisible church on earth.

Roman Catholic Emphasis

The Roman Catholic Church holds to what might be accurately defined as the "Petrine view" of the church. That is to say, as successor to Peter's throne, she claims a clearly defined concept of the body of Christ that is visible for all to see. Adhering strongly to a visible doctrine of the church, the Roman Catholic stand makes it quite clear that as the body of Christ, she is called upon to make a public and recognizable confession of her faith to the world as the church of Christ. These two aspects of visibility, public and recognizable, "are termed respectively, 'material' and 'formal' visibility by Catholic theologians. The material visibility of the Church involves no more than that it must ever be a public, not a private, profession; a society manifest to the world, not a body whose members are bound by some secret tie. Formal visibility is more than this. It implies that in all ages the true Church of Christ will be easily recognizable for that which it is, viz., as the Divine society of the Son of God, the means of salvation offered by God to men; that it possesses certain attributes which so evidently postulate a Divine origin that all who see it must know it comes from God."[2] Hence, formal visibility of the church for Roman Catholics will be seen in terms of unity, sanctity, catholicity, and apostolicity. These attributes or "notes" of the church connote to the believer that these are the marks of the true visible church of Jesus Christ and that he belongs to the *communio sanctorum* of this church. "Today, when Catholics and non-Catholics are coming together in various meetings, the basis of discussion is the ecclesiology of the New Testament and of the early centuries, rather than the notes, or marks, of the Church. Nevertheless, the attributes of unity, catholicity, holiness, and apostolicity could be the topic of a fruitful dialogue, even if they are not always accepted as valid marks of the true Church."[3] This post-Vatican II elasticity of attitude is welcomed, but the Catholic believer continues to receive assurance in practice that the property of visibility belongs to the church on earth (*ecclesia militans*).

The above viewpoint leads to the stand that the church is the necessary means of salvation (*extra ecclesiam nulla salus*). However, it is also true that Roman Catholic *ecclesiology* does not wish to say emphatically that such a position excludes the possibility that some might be saved who are outside the visible communion of the church. There is the possibility for justification for even those outside the church who perform acts "of perfect charity and of contrition. Whoever, under the impulse of actual grace, elicits these acts receives immediately the gift of sanctifying grace, and is numbered among the children of God."[4] And yet the fact remains, such acts of charity and contrition from the Roman Catholic view will include, even if delayed a while, the desire for incorporation within the visible church. While any concept of the invisible church is rejected, there is evidence here that the idea of invisibility is not altogether excluded in the Petrine understanding of the body of Christ (*corpus Christi*). This fact is made even more explicit in current reference to those outside the visible communion of the Roman Catholic Church as "separated brethren." In any case, however, the Roman Church essentially remains and holds to the familiar saying of Cyprian, who spoke in behalf of the visible church, "You cannot have God for your father unless you have the Church for your mother."[5]

Protestant Polemic

The Reformers amplified Augustine's concept of the invisible church[6] in their polemic with the Roman Catholic emphasis

upon the visibility of the church. The strength and weakness
of Protestant ecclesiology lies within the crux of this distinction. Wycliffe, Luther,[7] Zwingli, and Calvin in stressing the
visible/invisible distinction in view of Augustine and the New
Testament were attempting to say that such a delineation exists
in the "catholic history" of the Christian church. Whether this
is the case or not is debatable. Nevertheless, it is clear that the
Reformers were aware of the apparent difference between the
essence of the church and their experience of the church in
their time. The accent upon the visible/invisible division was
aimed primarily to point out this wide difference between what
the church claimed to be and what it actually was in practice.
The visible church designated what was incomplete, corrupt,
unholy, and external, whereas the invisible church pointed to
what was complete, incorruptible, holy, and internal. This notion pointed to the church within a church. In fact, it seemed
to indicate or imply that there was a kind of Platonic essence
or ideal of which the visible church was unfortunately only a
partial and defective image. Thus the "true" church was a
purely transcendent and heavenly reality, while the existing
and earthly church was imperfect and impure.

The Reformers, of course, in making the distinction of the
visible/invisible church were not interested in creating two
churches—one visible and the other invisible—but unfortunately the ambiguity of these terms suggested such a division
to later followers and opponents of the Protestant movement.
Calvin, like Cyprian, spoke of the church as the "mother" of
believers. Calvin rightly placed emphasis upon the visible
church in its function of bearing and nourishing believers as is
necessary for salvation.[8] Calvin correctly saw that the concept
of the invisible church is beyond the visible church and therefore beyond ecclesiology insofar as the empirical reality of the
church on earth is concerned, but that nevertheless there remained, to use Luther's term, a "hidden nature" (*abscondita*)
about the church in its totality as the body of Christ. Hence, the
use of the invisible concept of the church was designed to bring

out this "hidden nature" but was not meant to suggest the idea of two churches. Calvin, as well as Luther, was adamantly clear at this point in his ecclesiology, as they both were in their Christology. There could no more be two churches than two Christs.

The Scottish divines, for example, also were keen enough to catch the implicit organic tension involved in the visible/invisible distinction of the church. They thought of the church as a *coetus hominum*. It was unthinkable that the soul and body can be separated in a *coetus* (an "assemblage") such as the church. They reasoned "(*a*) that the Church is necessarily embodied, (*b*) that the embodiment is always a good in itself, (*c*) that the embodiment is nevertheless liable to disease, and (*d*) that the radical surgery the cure may entail is the work of Christ, the Head, by the Holy Spirit working through the ministry. The 'Kirk Malignant' is not really another Church at all, for the Church is one; it is, rather, a parasite on the True Church. It could not live by itself, for it is its life to feed upon the Church it seeks to devour. All this was consonant with Calvin's ecclesiology."[9] It is with this background that the Reformation must be rightly understood and from which the impetus for the distinction between the visible/invisible arose with its later harmful connotation that possibly two churches exist with one Head.[10] It is this misunderstanding of the Reformers that is usually attacked by Orthodox and Roman Catholics.

Like the Roman Catholics, Calvin viewed the visible church on earth (to use the Pauline phrase) as the body of Christ (*corpus Christi*). This implied that the church was a type of incarnation but not identical with the purity of our Lord's incarnation.[11] "Thus in the ministry of the Church there takes place a condescension of God to our world similar to that implied in the incarnation of the Word in Jesus Christ. The condescension of God in the institution of the Church is a type of the former original condescension."[12] Calvin, like the Roman Catholics, is certainly not concerned with developing a doc-

trine of two churches.[13] Calvin and the other Reformers sought
to confront the visible or empirical church of their time with
the realization that there is an *abscondita* or *invisibilis* to
human awareness regarding the empirical reality of the
church. Therefore, the visible church is not altogether identical
with the body of Christ in its totality. The truly visible church
is known only to God in its entirety, while from our standpoint
this realization, due to limitations of a human character, will
find this picture of the one visible church partially eclipsed.
This is exactly what the visible/invisible distinction is attempting to describe to us. This distinction should not be interpreted
in a polemical fashion (even though this is what friends and
foes of the Reformers tend to do even to this day), or as the
difference between the true and the false church, but rather
as what is characteristic of the finite nature of the human perception of the visible church, which will always be less than
perfect.[14] To put it positively, the Protestant insistence would
be upon the Pauline emphasis on the unique singularity and
oneness of the Lord and Head of the church, namely, Christ.
Where he is acknowledged and confessed as the Head, there
will be found his body, the visible and gathered church of our
common Lord and Savior Jesus Christ.

Orthodox Position

If Roman Catholicism is said to be Petrine in character and
Protestantism is identified as Pauline, it can then be said that
Eastern Orthodoxy is marked by a Johannine nature.[15] What
does this imply? It should first be acknowledged that such a
characterization as the above is fluid rather than static. What
needs to be seen is that it is not merely by chance that Eastern
Orthodoxy has been closely associated with the name of John.
Actually, "the Eastern Church has reserved the name of 'theo-
logian' peculiarly for three sacred writers of whom the first is
St. John, most 'mystical' of the four Evangelists; the second, St.
Gregory Nazianzen, writer of contemplative poetry; and the

third, St. Symeon, called 'the new Theologian,' the singer of union with God."[16] Eastern Orthodoxy with its Johannine character emphasizes the visible nature of the church, but places it within a mystical context. This mystical aspect associated with visibility is somewhat akin to the concern of Protestants interested in the *abscondita* or *invisibilis* of the one church of Jesus Christ.

Orthodoxy would insist on the fact that unity belongs to the one church, which essentially cannot be divided by human controversies. Man cannot really divide God and his truth, and then through his efforts later restore them to unity.[17] Orthodoxy thus thinks of itself as bearing witness to the undivided, unbroken tradition of the one church created at Pentecost. Orthodoxy prefers to allow the Holy Spirit, the inspirer of the church and the indwelling Spirit of Christ, to judge the external as well as internal visibility of the *ecclesia militans* on earth. Having said this, Eastern Orthodoxy does go on to assert that the true and actual visibility of the church within human perception is seen in the Eucharistic worship, set aside and blessed not by human hands but through the mystical act of the Holy Spirit. This pneumatological accent upon the Spirit as found in The Gospel According to John, coupled with the apophatic nature of its theology in general, points toward an ecclesiology that is basically mystical, shrouded in wonder and mystery. In short, Eastern Orthodoxy holds to the visible but *mystical* body of Christ.

Each of the major Christian traditions discussed has struggled with this problem of the church's visibility and invisibility, with the tendency of emphasizing one and neglecting the other. We can begin to see that there is inherent in this distinction a tension which cannot be neatly dismissed or ignored. The problem rightly seen belongs to all the traditions within the total history of the Christian church. The choice of terms has been an unfortunate one, for it suggests the idea of a church within a church.[18] It suggests either a Platonic vision of the church or points to a division or disunity, as if one

church is truer and more authentic than the other. This, however, is really not the case, since the church, like the Godhead,
is one; also, Jesus is one, our baptism is one, and our hope is
one (Eph. 4:1–7). If such is the case, then the gathering of
those in his name must also be one as well if it is indeed to
be the *communio sanctorum*. Thus due to polemical controversies in the life and history of the Christian church attached
to the visible/invisible distinction, what was intended originally
to be a positive and exploratory attempt to describe the *totality*
of the *communio sanctorum* became instead an ecclesiastical
battlefront.

If the church is to be understood as a type of the incarnation,
then its nature must be a mysterious, undivided, and *visible*
whole. The New Testament knows no distinction between a
visible and an invisible church.[19] The Christian community
(*ecclesia* or *communio sanctorum*) is as visible and bodily as
the individual Christian. However, the complete realization
or perception of this must be seen eschatologically, which
means that from our human perspective her visibility will be
eclipsed from our sight, even though in her entirety she is seen
and known by the Head of the church.[20]

Due to the misunderstanding of the term "invisible" and the
polemical connotation associated with it, it would perhaps be
wisest to drop this term. The accent should be upon the term
"visibility," but allowing this term wider flexibility and coverage than its present fixed and limited boundaries. In other
words, "as we look from Him, the actual unity of the Church
will certainly be visible at a greater or lesser distance."[21] Thus,
with this proper stress upon visibility, we will be less prone
to escape our responsibility of working toward the visible
unity of the divided church. The church on earth (*ecclesia
militans*) is no mere shadow of an invisible reality out yonder.
She is, rather, the firstfruits and the instrument of God's gracious will for his purpose to re-create the human race to become his suitable partner. He does this through the effectual
work of the Holy Spirit, who by dwelling in the church is pre-

paring her for her wedding day.[22] It is precisely at this point
that the emphasis on the *mystical* aspect of the body of Christ
found so clearly in Eastern Orthodoxy makes a welcome contribution.[23] For in its depth, this note of mystery and awe due to
the indwelling of the Holy Spirit enables us to see that hu-
manly speaking we are never able to draw our own confessional circle either qualitatively or quantitively and thereby
pronounce that this is the visible church in its totality. Instead,
the church needs to relax at this very point of her limitation,
and to take courage and hope from the fact that she nevertheless has been already sighted, picked, and is being prepared to
become the only bride of Him who is the Groom and Head of
the *communio sanctorum*.[24]

All future conversations among the traditions must continue
in love and in humility before the amazing fact of God's *communio sanctorum,* the *ecclesia militans.* This involves a further
uncovering of the layers of pride which imprison our respective traditions—working, hoping, and praying together until
that day when the *Una, Sancta, Catholica,* and *Apostolica* of
the One, Visible Church of Jesus Christ, the mystical body of
Him who is the Head, might be known to us as fully as she
is already known to him.

Chapter VI

The Hierarchy and the Laity

"Layman Charges New Minister," reads the headline in a noted Protestant religious journal,[1] describing the unusual act of a parishioner challenging a newly called pastor before the congregation as he assumes his duties in that church. In a similar vein, Cardinal Saliége is reported to have said of his church: "The wretched theologians! They have forgotten two things—the laymen and the Holy Spirit."[2] It is not an exaggeration to say that Protestants of an earlier day no less than Roman Catholics evicted the laity from their clerical realm. Today, we are witnessing the ascendancy of the laity in Western Christendom, a theological factor to which Eastern Christendom has borne witness throughout the centuries. This is not to say that Eastern Christendom is free from clericalism; unfortunately it is not. In comparison to the West, however, the East has been more faithful to the concept of the priesthood of all believers.

Primacy of the Laity

Historically, Orthodoxy has stood for the primacy of the laity. The survival of the churches of Eastern Christendom is due primarily to the laity's conscious conviction that the church belongs to and exists for all the people, not simply for the clergy alone. Each believer, each faithful member of the community, is entrusted in his baptism with the advancement and safekeeping of the sacred tradition. With this unadorned

78

conviction, both the simple and the sophisticated among the laity have contributed enormously to the survival of Orthodoxy against the innumerable dangers and difficulties which have sought to crush and to subvert her witness. Thus, to those of us who saw and heard him, it was a significant tribute to the fidelity of the laity in Orthodoxy that the Greek Orthodox lay theologian Prof. Nikos Nissiotis preached from John Calvin's historic pulpit in the Church of Saint Pierre in Geneva not long ago. His presence was a witness to the important role that laity can fill in Orthodoxy. Orthodoxy regards all its adherents as active participants in the life and mission of the church. Unfortunately, the acknowledged theological illiteracy in many quarters of contemporary lay Orthodoxy has contributed to today's unhealthy imbalance, similar in scope to that found among Protestants and Roman Catholics. While there are many social, political, and ecclesiastical causes behind this factor, only the theological cause for the imbalance will be discussed here.

Ordination into the laity for the East as well as the West begins at baptism. The theological import of baptism has often been lost in Christendom by both the clergy who administer baptism and the laity who receive it. The Orthodox are more aware than the West that baptism implies entrance and acceptance into the community. The East views the church as the *ordained community* called out to be the people (*laos*) of God, and set aside for a sacred and holy use by God.[3] Hence the designation of their priestly character or what is more familiarly referred to as "the priesthood of all believers." From a Biblical standpoint, it is difficult to uncover the notion of a secular or profane concept of laity as practiced in the "split-level fellowships" of our churches today.[4] Biblically, "laity" implies "priestly" in an inclusive sense, but by the end of the fourth century the primacy of the laity was being challenged as class distinctions formed within the community. Within the church the laity and the clergy sought their separate ways. Today, we are living under the shadow of this cleavage begun in the age of Constantine. Our current post-Constantine era is in search of its identity as the people of God. "It was the lay people themselves who relinquished their dignity as a universal priesthood, and then inevitably the bishops became more and more the point of concentration of the sacred, the priestly, 'the consecrated.' A distance was formed by the indigence, the progressive impoverishment of the laity, by its terrible refusal of the gifts of the Holy Spirit."[5] According to Orthodox theologian Evdokimov, "this was the great 'treason of the laity,' a betrayal of their priestly character. Of the two poles of the *laos,* the People of God, one was that of the Christian king who protected the Church and was called 'the exterior bishop' and 'ecumenical deacon' (title of the Byzantine emperors), and the other was that of the monk, who lived in the things of God. These two poles safeguarded the charismatic dignity of the laity; but the rest, what was between these two poles, fell into a vacuum, now really *profane.*"[6] Both East and West in varying degrees are the heirs of this development. Today, Orthodox differ only in degree from Western churchmen in the realization of the "priesthood of all believers" as a living experience in the life of their respective churches.[7]

Nevertheless, Orthodoxy has made a distinct contribution theologically in understanding the meaning of a vibrant laity. For example, Orthodoxy follows the sacrament of Baptism immediately with another, the sacrament of Holy Chrism. These two sacraments are yoked together as sacraments of entrance into the church. Baptism restores the individual to his true human nature which has been obscured by sin, while Chrismation gives the power and grace for the individual layman to act as a Christian in life, thereby fulfilling his citizenship in the Kingdom of God.[8] Anointment by the chrism (Holy Myron in the Oriental tradition) is comparable to the practice of confirmation in the West, and for the Easterner, it represents specifically a baptism of the Spirit preceded by the baptism with water. The sign of the cross is made with holy oil (the chrism or myron) on all parts of the body (usually that of an infant), thereby symbolizing the tongues of fire at Pentecost. "It is accompanied by the sacred formula: 'Seal of the gift of the Holy Spirit.' It is therefore in his entire being that every lay person is sealed with the gifts; he is an entirely *charismatic* being."[9] This recognition that the baptized person is a charismatic being is a vivid sign that he now belongs to the hieratic or priestly order in the community. From this common status of equality through the twofold sacrament, some are chosen to be deacons, presbyters, and bishops. These latter offices or orders are functional in nature, but in no way do they separate the ontological oneness enjoyed by the hierarchy and laity who share in a common priesthood through their baptism.[10] Every bishop as well as every member of the church is first and primarily a lay priest.

It is precisely because of the theological faithfulness of Orthodoxy in viewing each baptized member as a lay priest that Orthodoxy expects its membership to be theologians. That is to say, the followers are to consider themselves called out to verify and to purify the authentic witness of the church in any given age. Thus the laymen, as well as the clergy, as members of the church are entrusted with the keeping of the faith from any external or internal rift. For instance, members of the parish are expected to watch closely the performance of a newly installed priest to see whether he conducts the worship service correctly. Support for such observation is expressed in the well-known encyclical letter of the Eastern Patriarchs (1848), according to which "the guardian of Orthodoxy is the body of the Church, i.e., the members themselves."[11] Other illustrations of this primacy exercised by the laity are seen in their rejection of the Council of Florence (1438–1439); also, in the necessary approval from the laity for any clerical candidate to be ordained in any of the orders of the hierarchy. In short, the Orthodox tradition clearly reminds us, in the light of our current ecumenical concerns, that the authority of the

church resides with the conscientious pleroma of the people
of God, a universal priesthood, consecrated through the sacraments of Baptism and Holy Chrism.[12]

The Significance of Clerical Ordination

Why, then, is there the need for ordination of a clerical class
in Orthodoxy as well as in Western Christendom? If our priesthood is assured in our baptism, is there a need for further ordinations within the community of believers? Both Eastern and
Western Christendom have long believed that universal priesthood initiated through baptism implies in no way any opposition to the functional priesthood of the clergy. From the
Orthodox standpoint, "the Church has received a hierarchical
structure from the institution of the college of the Twelve in
conformity with the divine plan. The People of God is differen-
tiated by God in its 'priestly principle,' by means of charismatic
ministries. The episcopate is chosen from among the people; it
is of its priestly flesh and blood; it does not form a structure
above, for it is an organic part of the body, an ontological unity
of all its members."[13]

One is therefore ordained to the episcopate to celebrate the
ministries originally entrusted to the apostles; hence the symbolic reasoning for the episcopate to be in apostolic succession.
"The sacramental power of celebrating the mysteries, and
above all, of being an apostolic witness to the eucharist, and
the power of promulgating doctrinal definitions—*charisma
veritatis certum*—belong to the episcopate in virtue of the
apostolicity of the Church."[14] The clergy are therefore dependent upon the *laos* and at the same time remind the *laos*
of their historic continuity and destiny as the people of God.

The dependence of the episcopate upon the laity is seen at
each stage of the hierarchical structure of the episcopate—
deacons, priests, and bishops. For example, the ordination of a
priest has the following procedure: The candidate is brought
to the center of the congregation. Usually a subdeacon will

ask if the ordination may proceed, and the congregation is
expected to reply by saying, "*Axios*," or "He is worthy" (to be
ordained); a unanimous reply is necessary, for if there are any
dissenting voices, the service cannot proceed. "The assembled
clergy are then asked the same question, and the same reply
is awaited. After unanimous consent has been secured the
candidate is three times conducted round the communion
table and then brought to the bishop who lays his hands upon
the candidate's head and recites the following prayer: 'The
grace divine which always healeth that which is infirm, and
completeth that which is wanting, is prophesying (or is desig-
nating) (name) the most devout deacon, to be a priest.
Wherefore let us pray for him that the grace of the all-Holy
Spirit may come upon him.' "[15] The bishop then raises the
newly ordained priest to his feet and proclaims, "*Axios*" three
times, followed each time with a response from the laity in the
same manner, thus symbolizing that the final act of confirmation is left to the will of the community.

Orthodoxy emphasizes the communal nature of the church
in which the clerical ordination finds its meaning and identity.
Unlike Roman Catholics, who support the call of the ordinand
by the Holy Spirit with the laying on of hands by a bishop,
or Protestants, who associate the call to serve with a subjective
inner urging by the Holy Spirit, the Orthodox by virtue of this
communal nature find the call of the Holy Spirit upon the
candidate expressed in the unanimous approval of the individual by the community of believers gathered together for
the service. "When the Bishop proclaims 'The Divine grace is
prophesying' he confirms the fact of divine election, and he
seals it by the laying on of hands. The Divine will is manifest
when the congregation unanimously declares that the candidate is worthy to be ordained."[16] Clearly, the primacy of the
laity is asserted, with the communal nature of the church preserved through clerical ordination; the clergy maintain the
continuity of the fellowship in faithful remembrance of its
apostolic tradition. Protestants, however, would differ with

the Orthodox (Roman Catholics and Anglicans too) by insist-
ing upon the priority of faithfulness to apostolic doctrine vs.
apostolic succession as the key to determining the validity of
one's ordination.[17] In practice, ordination for Protestants and
for Orthodox is left in the hands of the community. Of course,
the final question of validity rests with the transcendent judgment of God who alone knows the heart of each candidate.

The clergy are ordained then to continue the apostolic tradition which is the mainspring of the community. The perpetua-
tion of the apostolic tradition is most evident in the celebration
of the Eucharist, for which purpose the newly ordained priest
has been selected by the community. His clerical ordination
enables him to lead the community in this sacerdotal function
which unites priest and people in their mutual calling as the
people of God.

Even here in the celebration of the Eucharist, the priest is
aware that he has been set apart only functionally from the
people and remains ontologically very much at one with them.
Therefore, the laity must be present during the Eucharistic
service, for without them he is unable to celebrate the Eucharist. As church father John Chrysostom has said: " 'It is not the
priest alone who renders thanks [he is speaking of the Eucha-
rist]; it is the whole people.' The Eucharist is celebrated by
the whole people, but only when its chief is at its head, for
without him there is no people; in the same way, there is no
head unless the people are present also."[18] It is therefore important for us in the West to realize that for the Orthodox, this
"con-celebration by the laity is effective and real, not ceremonial. In the liturgy the laity are not passive—for those
whom God has appointed to the ministry of the royal priesthood cannot be passive."[19] Thus the priest and the people, in
harmony with one another, manifest their need for the other
around the Eucharistic banquet which distinguishes the charismatic nature of the *ecclesial* community as opposed to other
organizing communities.

The significance, then, of clerical ordination is to remind the church of her heritage and her destiny as the people of God. The function of the clergy is primarily an instrumental role in proclaiming the grace of God, administering his saving and healing power, teaching and disciplining within the commandments of God. The clergyman does not have any authority in himself, only through his office which the Holy Spirit has entrusted to him with the approval of the *laos*. In practice, then, the priest "has the power to teach, but only inasmuch as he teaches the Tradition of the Church, and is completely obedient to it. He has the *power to* celebrate, but again, only inasmuch as he fulfills the eternal Priesthood of Christ Himself. He is bound—totally and exclusively—by the Truth which He represents and, thus, can never speak or command in his own name."[20]

As Father Alexander Schmemann points out: "The conclusion is clear: there is no opposition between clergy and laity in the Church. Both are essential. The Church as a totality is *Laity* and the Church as a totality is the Inheritance, the Clergy of God. And in order to be this, there must exist within the Church the distinctions of functions, of ministries that complete one another. The clergy are *ordained* to make the Church the gift of God—the manifestation and communication of His Truth, grace and salvation to men. It is their sacred function, and they fulfill it only in complete obedience to God. The laity are *ordained* to make the Church the acceptance of that gift, the 'Amen' of mankind to God. They equally can fulfill their function only in complete obedience to God. It is the same obedience: to God and to the Church that establishes the harmony between clergy and laity, making them *one body*, growing into the fulness of Christ."[21] The primacy of the laity no less than the significance of clerical ordination must be seen, then, not in juxtaposition to each other but as organically related in a single fabric, and recognizable to insider and outsider alike as the people of God. Such a viewpoint can

be acceptably advanced for Protestants as well as for Orthodox.

Toward a Fourfold Ministry

The discussion thus far in this chapter has been an attempt
to show how clergy and laity are integrally united as *the laity*
or people of God. Their ministry is based upon this ontological
oneness, a theological oneness which the East, in comparison
to the West, held as a model. In practice, both the East and
the West have been suffering from clericalism, a tendency
that is out of harmony with the spirit of *laos* and ultimately
fatal to the health of the body of Christ as a living organism.
To remedy this trend, the traditional structures (or orders) of
ministry must be rediscovered in the West as well as the East,
for the sake of restoring a *unified* theological concept of *laos*.

The proposal for a unified concept of *laos* begins with a
recovery of what it means to be baptized into the laity. The
primary step toward a fourfold ministry begins with ordination
to *the laity* as experienced through the sacraments of Baptism
and Holy Chrism (confirmation). Both Protestants and Roman
Catholics are currently reshaping their understanding of confirmation. Theologically, the uniting of baptism and confirmation will mutually strengthen the implications and the responsibility of baptism itself as a meaningful commitment to the
community of the faithful. Periodically, the community should
make provisions or opportunities for the confessional renewal
of one's baptismal vows in public. In a real sense, this is done
actually each time the believer participates in the Eucharist.
However, definite public occasions should be made possible
in the life of the community in which "clergy" and "laity" can
witness to each other of their essential oneness as the body of
Christ and recognize their mutual ministry in a unified way to
the world at large. This first step can then be considered the
cornerstone of a unified fourfold ministry.

Max Thurian's thought-provoking discussion of new approaches to the sacrament of confirmation argues for a baptism of the Spirit to be viewed as a single and continuous event begun with the baptism by water. As Thurian expresses it, "the character of the seal, of baptism in the Spirit, is not repeated; in fact, the elements of baptism in water and in the Spirit which signify redemption, regeneration, entry into the Church, the indelible marking for the kingdom—these are not to be repeated. There is but one sacrament of salvation in Christ and of integration into the Body of Christ through the Holy Spirit and unto the Day of Redemption. But it is possible to renew a consecration in the royal priesthood of the people of God and to orient it specifically to a service."[22] Thus Thurian proposes a confirmation liturgy which would recall the baptismal vows made either for (in the case of infancy) or by (in case of an adult) the candidate. While Thurian's proposal is indeed commendable, would it not be theologically and Biblically more accurate to refer to such a confessional liturgy of affirmation as a "Liturgy of Baptismal Renewal," dropping the term "confirmation" altogether? The term denotes in far too many Western churches an erroneous sense of "commencement and graduation" from the *laos*. Such a renaming must stress the singleness of the baptismal act and thereby avoid the unwelcome possibilities of "rebaptism" or "second baptism" as practiced among some groups, thus undermining the validity of the sacramental act when it was initially performed. Such practices can only spread confusion and misunderstanding among Christians.

In addition to this initial and primary ordination to the *laos* through baptism, the early Christian community saw the need for other types of ordination in order to fulfill its ministry and maintain both the unity and the diversity of the *laos*. Hence the traditional clerical offices of bishops, presbyters (priests or elders), and deacons arose in the life of the early church. These clerical offices were filled from among members in the community and with their approval. There is ample New Testament backing and scholarly research to validate the basic forms of polity practiced today by the several traditions in the processes for selecting their clergy.[23] It is important to assert that each of the offices and the subsequent ordinations were designed for the *functional purposes* of guiding the *laos* in its need for continuity amid inevitable change. Ordination itself was the act of a public declaration that an individual had been selected by the community and given a place (an order) structurally within the community. These clerical offices constitute the second, third, and fourth phases of a fourfold ministry.

These clerical offices have by their very nature given a hierarchical structure to the church, but within the context of the primacy of the *laos*. This theological fact must be clearly before us as we consider the office of bishop. As Theodore of Mopsuestia has expressed it, "the bishop is 'the mouthpiece of the Church' for it is through him and in him that the ministry of the priesthood accomplished by God's people is manifested. This means that every Christian present, as a member of God's people, is cooperating with the bishop whenever he accomplishes a liturgical act. . . . The feeling is deeply rooted in the Orthodox Church (though it is not always translated in actual life) that the bishop or priest cannot celebrate the Eucharist without the people, and the people cannot celebrate the Eucharist without the bishop. . . . The priesthood belongs to God's people as a whole, and every member plays an active part in the liturgy as co-minister with his bishop."[24] Therefore, it is essential in the episcopal ordination of a bishop that the final *axios*, the final *amen*, be reserved to the *laos*, for the candidate to the office is thereby reminded vividly of the sacred trust the people have placed in him to be their spokesman. The idea of a passive *laos* is contrary to the universal priesthood which shares actively in the ministry of the community with its bishop.

The functional role of the bishop in the community is to provide the focal point of unity and communion with one another in the name of Christ. For the Orthodox, "the hierarchy in the Church is not, except in the field of Canon Law, divided into grades. The hierarchical constitution of the Church as a community is summed up in the relationship between the Head and the Body, the bishop and the congregation, the two terms of the relationship together forming the community which is the Mystical Body of Christ and whose Head is Christ. This relation is not juridical in character but sacramental."[25] In the thoughts of Ignatius, "there exists an inseparable relationship between the bishop and the Eucharist. Unity with the bishop and unity with each other in the one bread within the altar is precisely one identical reality."[26] This sacramental and ascetic presence of the bishop has the force of uniting the community.

Unity, then, in the bishop "is an image of the Church's unity with Christ, and of Christ's with the Father. Subjugation to the bishop is an icon of subjugation to God, Christ, and each other."[27] Hence, the office of the bishop provides a necessary center for the corporate life of the community in Christ. The bishop, and at the same time the presbytery and diaconate, have been entrusted by the faithful to administer correctly the corporate sacraments of the church. In this context, Ignatius can be understood when he says that without bishop, presbytery, and diaconate there can be no church, no local community, no *laos*.[28] In short, it can be observed that the hierarchy and the laity are intricately interwoven and interdependent upon one another.

The office of presbyter is similar to that of the bishop but does not carry with it the power to ordain to the clerical priesthood. From this viewpoint, the presbyter or priest is the elder representative of the bishop within the immediate community. He is the extended arm of the bishop whose rule is usually over a larger area. The chief duty of the priest through word and sacrament is to nurture and to guide the community to be indeed the people of God. His task is to preserve constantly the peace and unity of the body "by keeping beyond its limits the evil spirit of division and of individualistic and ulterior motivations. The clergy are not over the local body, but are themselves members of the local body who are given the special charisma of being the center of unity and the regulating force which protects and increases (Eph. 4:11–13) the life of corporate love in Christ. To Polycarp, Ignatius writes, 'Maintain your position with all care . . . preserve the unity than which nothing is better' (Pol. 1)."[29] The presbyters or priests are those members of the *laos* whose charisma is to govern, teach, and lead in worship the sacramental life of the community.

The diaconate is the extended arm of the priesthood as the priesthood is the arm of the episcopate. While the diaconate is an ordained office and is grouped with the clerical offices, in practice it has been almost absorbed by the laity because of its closeness to the people. Some Orthodox feel that the office of deacon is actually an anachronism today in the life of the church. It seems that the deacon's role "has been absorbed in its liturgical aspect by the priest on the one hand, and in its social aspect by the laity on the other. This has made the deacon an anachronism."[30] Nevertheless, there has been a revival of interest in the diaconate in both the East and the West to provide those who wish the opportunity (if given the approval of the *laos*) to dedicate themselves to a compassionate service of welfare to those in need both physically and spiritually.[31] Perhaps the diaconate for both Orthodox and Protestants (and Roman Catholics) might become the experimental arm of the church's ministry—a flexible and versatile Christian "peace corps"—that will capture the spirit and zest of both young and old who wish to have some specialized ministry for the sake of the church's total mission. Hence their distinction from the laity at large would be, as in the case of bishops and priests, solely functional in terms of their particular assignments.

Our discussion, in summary, reveals that Christendom, in both the East and the West, has suffered from a dichotomy within the people of God. Orthodoxy, Protestantism, and Roman Catholicism are rediscovering for tomorrow's Christianity the meaning of *laos* in their respective traditions. Orthodoxy in particular has had a rich theological heritage in supporting theologically the primacy of the laity in its interdependent relationship with the hierarchy. The significance of clerical ordination serves to remind the *laos* of its identity and its ministry as centered in the celebration of the Eucharist. The churches, East and West, in renewing their traditional structure of orders will affirm once again that the church is neither a clerical nor a lay institution but certainly both. Above all, the church is a charismatic organism which listens with an eschatological ear to the voice of the Holy Spirit, the Universal Bishop of the people of God, on their earthly pilgrimage toward the goal of their priestly calling in Jesus Christ.

Chapter VII

Church, State,
and Social Consciousness

For the Western observer, the relationship of church and state in Eastern Orthodoxy may appear as a puzzling picture in need of deciphering and explanation. Such a puzzle, for example, is the activity of Archbishop Makarios, who functions simultaneously as the head of the Cyprus Orthodox Church and as the secular President of Cyprus. In the reported words of Archbishop Iakovos of the Greek Orthodox Archdiocese of North and South America, this single rule of church and state under Makarios may seem "strange and untenable" to the West, but the role is "eminently explainable and consistent." According to Archbishop Iakovos, "during the centuries of Turkish rule over traditional Hellenic territories in Greece, Asia Minor, Cyprus and the Mediterranean islands, the Greek people looked for ethnic leadership to the church. . . . In assuming their roles as Ethnarchs, the Greek Orthodox Church leaders, and the faithful priests of Orthodoxy, are certainly not instigators nor politically ambitious troublemakers. They are simply doing what their people want them to do." Archbishop Iakovos is referring to the fact that four fifths of the 450,000 Cypriots are Orthodox Greeks and actually look to the church for guidance, since the church has remained faithful under centuries of turmoil and persecution. This tradition of clerical leadership is merely continued as the Cypriots follow Archbishop Makarios in secular as well as church matters.

Actually, this role of clerical leadership in secular areas of life is contrary to the historic Byzantine understanding of church-state relations. The Cyprus situation illustrates the fact that under the Turkish sultan and his establishment of ethnarchs, the church's influence was paradoxically heightened by her forced concern in secular affairs. As a result, the Ecumenical Patriarch in Constantinople found himself in an unusual twofold office (both political and ecclesiastical). Makarios inherits this imposed dual position which is actually quite different from the accepted Byzantine stance on church-state relations.

Church-State: A Symphonic Relationship

The proper Byzantine understanding of church-state relations might be described as a dyarchy or symphonia between two coordinated powers. This pointed to the *sacerdotium* rule of the patriarch and the *imperium* rule of the emperor, synchronized in harmonious fashion. This symphony of patriarch and emperor symbolized the victory of Christ over the world. Byzantine history reveals that the harmonics of this symphonic relation could not be maintained.

According to the Sixth Novella, dated March 16, A.D. 535, during the rule of Justinian, citizens on heaven and on earth are united under a single monarch. Church and state were thus no longer envisioned as two separate entities, but as one single society governed by two hierarchies—the ecclesiastical and the political. Neither the patriarch nor the emperor was permitted to wield exclusive power over his subjects. Although sound in theory, this system proved otherwise in practice.

The symphonic relationship implied an aesthetic elegance enhanced by a metaphysical ambiguity characteristic of Hellenic philosophic thought. From the Eastern standpoint, this was the best formula yet conceived; while theoretically sound, its practical application would afford flexibility in changing circumstances. This plan seemed to provide an adequate system in obedience to the command of Christ to "render there-

fore to Caesar the things that are Caesar's, and to God the
things that are God's" (Matt. 22:21). The realization of this
ideal scheme presupposes Christian perfection on the part of
the church and the state. Since such perfection is not evident,
the historic result has been and continues to be a perpetual
drama and battle between church and state.

There appear within the New Testament at least three basic
attitudes toward government: (1) that of viewing the state as
a divine institution (Rom. 13:1-7 and I Tim. 2:1-2); (2) that
of opposition to the state (Rev., ch. 13); and (3) that of acceptance of the state (Luke 7:1-10 and Matt. 22:16-22).
Whatever stance the church chooses in the situation, she
should be reminded of the New Testament view of history,
which is eschatological. Neglect of this eschatological perspective has led the church to erroneous solutions: "Either that the
Church tries to put itself in the place of the State: or else that
the State is simply accepted uncritically in all that it does, as
if there were no problem at all. Although the bearing of the
Church in the two cases is radically opposite, in both cases the
Church is guilty of the same fault: relinquishment of the New
Testament interpretation of the end-time."[1]

Historically, the Byzantine emperor was crowned by the
Patriarch of Constantinople (a practice begun in mid-fifth
century) and was thereby regarded as the Friend of Christ,
the Protector of Orthodoxy. To parallel this practice, a newly
elected patriarch was consecrated by the emperor's pronounc-
ing the words of institution: "This man is appointed Patriarch
of Constantinople by the grace of God and our imperial
authority which proceeds from the grace of God." Having
clarified each other's roles, they proceeded often to trespass in
each other's affairs. Of course, there can be no rigid separation
of the sacred and the secular; these areas are integrally related.
Mindful of this overlap, it is incorrect to categorize either the
Byzantine or Latin structure as exclusively caesaropapism or
papocaesarism respectively. Either case leads to gross simplifi-
cations regarding the East and the West. In Byzantine culture

it is more correct to state that the relation of the emperor to the patriarch and that of the secular to the spiritual was *interdependent*. The symphonic doctrine sought to recognize the common interest of the church and state in society. This recognition of common interest in turn has been the chief cause for disharmony and tension between church and state.

According to Eusebius of Caesarea, the ecclesiastical adviser to the Emperor Constantine, "the source of all authority in the universe, both religious and secular is God. The Divine Logos —that is, Christ—is the supreme priest and king on earth, uniting in himself both *regnum* and *sacerdotium*. When Christ left the world the power was divided into two spheres, the spiritual being assigned to his apostles and the civil authority to Caesar. And throughout their history the Byzantines believed that the emperor derived his authority directly from God; hence the title *Christos Kyriou*. It was the Byzantine view, furthermore, that the church hierarchy derived its authority from Christ through the Apostles. But this seeming indirection was, for the clergy, not a mark of inferiority; on the contrary, they could, in a certain sense, be considered even superior to the emperor because of the purely spiritual nature of their ecclesiastical authority."[2]

Ideally, the church and state should strengthen and honor each other's freedom and independence. Theoretically, Justinian's Sixth Novella viewed the church and state as gifts from God and hence subject to the will of God. The Novella did not anticipate that either power would politically interpret God's will to its own aggrandizement; to this end the Novella was not realistic.

Illustrations of Disharmony

In practice, Justinian's Sixth Novella has not been successfully carried out in Eastern Orthodoxy. Church and state relations historically have been less than a harmonious interdependence. Prior to Justinian and his Novella, the reign of

Constantine already was inclined to define the limits, responsibilities, and privileges of the church. The intervention of Emperor Constantine in the First Ecumenical Council at Nicaea (A.D. 325) set the tone for future disharmony between the church and state.

Constantine's involvement in the Arian controversy at Nicaea was primarily an expression of imperial concern for unity and peace throughout the Empire. His direct contacting of the principals related to the controversy, Arius and Alexander, illustrates this. To gain even greater control of the proceedings, he persuaded the synod of bishops to transfer their proposed meeting place from Ancyra to Nicaea. He then transformed the synod into a general council, and presided. By dominating the proceedings, Constantine determined the final outcome of the council. Constantine, in effect, considered himself to be a bishop "to oversee whatever is external to the Church" as recorded by Eusebius in the *Vita* and to see himself as the "head" of the church as well as the emperor of the state.

Without a doubt, Constantine viewed himself as a benevolent but nevertheless "absolutist emperor who had no intention of letting the Church operate independently of the State. Politically and otherwise, religion and the State were historically inseparable. Indeed, the unity of faith and culture was the basic premise of classical society. . . . The real choice was between an anti-Christian society and a Christianized society. The Church could not help but share this conception of things, and therefore could only accept and, more commonly, welcome the change of policy under Constantine."[3] As a result, the state embraced the church, and the church embraced the state for the mutual advantage of each. Constantine's action in the past makes it difficult to ascertain today where the jurisdiction of the one begins and the other ends, thus contributing to continual disharmony between the church and the state.

More serious than Constantine's intervention at Nicaea was the Chalcedonian tragedy which caused an internal split

among the Eastern Christians into Chalcedonians (dyophy-
sites) and pre- or non-Chalcedonians (monophysites). Pres-
sure from the Byzantine emperor Marcian (A.D. 450–457),
convener of the Fourth Council of Chalcedon, caused the
Council to accept the controversial *Tome* of Leo defining the
two natures of Christ. The non-Chalcedonians had considered
the matter of Leo's *Tome* at the Latrocinium (the council held
at Ephesus in A.D. 449), and had denied it a reading. The
coercion to accept it at Chalcedon (A.D. 451) through the
aggressive action of the emperor seemed unjust. As a consequence, these churchmen (Copts, Armenians, and Syrians)
refused to attend the Fourth Ecumenical Council of Chalcedon. Emperor Marcian and the Byzantine churchmen present
at Chalcedon then proceeded to treat these Oriental Orthodox
Christians (i.e., non-Chalcedonians) as outcasts. The entire
incident and resulting rift were filled with political overtones.
A recent statement issued from the first unofficial theological
consultation[4] since the schism between Chalcedonians and
non-Chalcedonian Orthodox is an attempt to heal this unfortunate historic wound.

Emperor Constantine's involvement in important dogmatic
controversies stemmed mainly from his image of himself as
Pontifex Maximus. Constantine combined in himself the Hellenistic idea of kingship (*basileia*) and the Roman (caesaro-
papistic) idea of the emperor as Pontifex Maximus (highest
priest).[5] The emperor as Pontifex Maximus acted as mediator
between man and God, "not in the sense that he 'initiates'
members of the Church into the Christian Mysteries, for this
is the superior function of the eternal priesthood of the
Church; but in the sense that through the christianization of
society, the welding together of the local communities of the
Church into a united Christendom, and the establishing of the
equilibrium and justice of the latter on Christian principles, he
'binds' (to use a word not unconnected, etymologically, with
'religion' itself) all his subjects to the Church and to the
Christian Way."[6] In short, the emperor as Pontifex Maximus

not only blurred any sharp distinction between church and
state but at the same time revealed an authentic concern for
mutual partnership and support. The reduction of state support in most areas of the world today illustrates the fact that
we live in a post-Constantine era, popularly described (but
inaccurately) as a post-Christian epoch.

Constantine displayed his ecclesiastical role in many ways,
a partnership that was not without mixed motives. He paid for
the copying of the Scriptures; he built churches, not only to
aid the church substantially but also as a means of extending
his imperial control over the church. The very aim of his building policy reflected his desire for promoting along parallel and
complementary lines both ecclesiastical unity and the ultimate
unity of the Empire itself.[7] From Constantine to Justinian these
interrelated purposes prevailed in their construction plans: to
further the one true faith, the accompanying imperial propa-
ganda, and the emperors' own wishes to leave behind lasting
monuments built under their leadership, as the Pontifex Maximus of God. Justinian expressed his political theology in his
Codex Justinianus, "We rule, by the authority of God, the
empire which has been entrusted to us by the majesty of
Heaven."[8]

Other practical acts in Constantine's program of Christianization were the influence of favorable legislation in behalf of
the church, the reduction of barbarous punishments, the tight-
ening of penalties for sexual offenses, provisions for Sunday,
the dispensing of many pagan ceremonies, and the closing of
pagan temples. In practice, Constantine's role was evangelistic;
he saw himself as the "bishop of those outside the church." He
felt his mission extended to all men. " 'God scattered the evil
powers that mankind might be recalled to true religion instructed through my agency.' Writing to Sapor, King of Persia,
he said: 'I am convinced that the greatest safety and prosperity
will be enjoyed everywhere when God through the pure and
righteous worship of the Christians and from their agreement
concerning the deity shall deign to draw all men unto Himself.'

And to the bishops at Tyre: 'Even the barbarians themselves now on account of me, the sincere servant of God, have recognized God and have learned to reverence Him who, as they realize from His very acts, protects me and everywhere cares for me.' "[9] Constantine took seriously his role not only as emperor but as Pontifex Maximus, and thereby became the evangelist par excellence of the Empire, with the general consent of the bishops through the land. Constantine would indeed have had a substantial reply to Donatus' famous remark made some years later in battle with Constantine's son: "What has the emperor to do with the Church?"[10] According to Constantine and his sons, the emperor had not only a great deal to do with the church but had pushed the church and the state well along dualistic and complementary lines of support (a symphonic duet) until Julian the Apostate[11] struck the decisive note of disharmony by reopening the pagan temples.

Turning from Constantine to later Byzantine history, we find that incidents have also occurred where the church sought greater control over the state. In the eleventh century, Michael Caerularius (1043) ascended the Patriarchal Throne of Constantinople and subordinated the powers of the state with his strong and aggressive personality.[12] In Russia, the Orthodox Church under Patriarch Nikon (1605–1681) caused considerable unrest with reform measures while the weaker emperor conceded leadership. Nikon attempted to establish the principle of spiritual superiority over the state and thus endangered the symphonic doctrine. Nikon based his authority on the Latin document *Donatio Constantini*,[13] which pointed to the alleged privileges given by Constantine the Great to Pope Sylvester I. The document was later proved false, and Nikon's argument for control was lost, but the note of disharmony had already been sounded by the senseless persecution of Old Believers (i.e., Old Ritualists), who refused to accept Nikon's reforms.

The spurious document *Donatio Constantini* was alien to the Byzantine mentality, contrary to the symphonic doctrine de-

veloped in the East. Nikon was condemned for his ruthless
rule by the Muscovite Synod at which the Eastern Patriarchs
were represented.[14] This later gave Peter the Great the opportunity to strike a further note of discord in the interest of the
autocratic state by discontinuing the patriarch's position in
Russia and replacing it with a synod under the influence of
German theoretician Puffendorf. This synod under the emperor's control lasted until November 4, 1917, with the election
of Tikhon as the first Russian patriarch since Nikon. While
there were many favorable aspects to the synod, it must be
said that its existence furthered the state's influence upon the
church. This influence still lingers in Russia today under Soviet
rule, where the church is subordinate to the wishes of the state.

In communist-governed lands, where a large number of
Orthodox Christians live, the church's freedom is limited by
the state. However, this curtailment varies within the different
countries depending upon their particular negotiations between the church and the state. For instance, the Rumanian
Orthodox Church, second largest church in Orthodoxy following the Russian Orthodox Church, is furnished with state
funds to maintain the clergy and the churches. In Russia, the
clergy and churches in contrast are supported on a voluntary
basis. However, in various parts of the Soviet Union, when it
serves their purposes, state funds are used to maintain the
upkeep of historic churches as found in the Kremlin. The Holy
See of the Armenian Apostolic Orthodox Church at Echmiad-
zin in the Soviet Republic of Armenia received some state aid
toward the restoration of the ancient monastery there.[15]

Now the above illustrations of cooperation between communist authorities and churchmen appear to contradict the
known hostility of the communist state toward the church.
Communism with its youthful history has in some remarkable
ways "come of age" in its opposition to religion. The teachings
of Lenin on the subject of religion experience constant re-
interpretation. For example, the present-day Communist ad-
heres to Lenin's teachings; found in a collection of his articles

entitled *On Religion* is the following exhortation: "We demand that religion be held a private affair so far as the state is
concerned. But by no means can we consider religion a private
affair so far as our Party is concerned."[16] The latter part of this
quote provides the communist official with an important loop-
hole (if he wishes to recognize it) to pursue an expedient
policy toward the prevailing church in his territory. In the
case of the Rumanians, communist officialdom recognizes that
the cultural roots of the people are embedded in the historic
Rumanian Orthodox Church. Instead of resisting this as
earlier, the state accepts and supports the church and gains
thereby the goodwill she needs among the people to advance
her policies.

It is not the intent of most communist countries to persecute
the church directly and thereby generate a "church of the cata-
combs." Rather, the aim is a more subtle and slower death for
the church through a less visible but nonetheless efficient
means of extinction. This is witnessed primarily in the state's
refusal of any form of Christian education for the youth, aside
from the very few who desire to enter a priestly vocation.
Education is the right of the state, not of the church. Hence,
at this very crucial point in the church's life, the state finds it
convenient and proper to advocate complete separation of
church and state, thereby undermining the future vitality of
the church. A small number of churches remain which are
dependent upon the state politically (and in some cases finan-
cially) as vestiges of the past, museumlike, where one is certainly free to enter (even to worship) and to leave in anony-
mity. In short, the churches in communist lands although
experiencing different treatments are basically regarded as
religious institutions subject to the powers and jurisdiction of
the state.

In the Middle Eastern countries, especially Egypt and Turkey, Islam presents a real threat to Eastern Christians. Ethiopia
should also be singled out here, not because it is a Muslim
country, but as an Orthodox nation in North Africa it is very

much aware of the advancing spirit of Islam. It can be said that Ethiopia and Greece are the only two nations whose monarchs are Orthodox, and the churches there enjoy a privileged position. Recently, Emperor Haile Selassie I of Ethiopia gave himself the significant title of "Defender of the Faith." This title takes on added significance in the light of the current Islamic wave of converts in Africa, which disturbs Ethiopian Christians.

In Egypt, the Coptic Orthodox Church with about four million adherents is conscious of its minority status and the consequent disadvantage of being Christian in an Islamic state.[17] While there is no doubt that Nasser's government has done and continues to do a great deal of good for his country, it has been partially at the expense of the non-Muslim minorities, most of whom are Orthodox Christians.

In Turkey, one is continually aware of the precarious situation of Ecumenical Patriarch Athenagoras I and his historic see in its relationships with the Turkish government. Historically, the struggle under Turkish rule has contributed to the interior decay within the very life of the church. "Intrigue, simony, and corruption dominated the higher administration of the Church. Each Patriarch of Constantinople on his election required a *berat* from the Sultan, as a confirmation of his spiritual and secular authority. It quickly became the regular practice for him to pay a large sum in order to obtain this official recognition, and it was therefore in the financial interests of the government to change the occupier of the see as frequently as possible. . . . Patriarchs were removed and reinstated with bewildering rapidity. 'Out of 159 Patriarchs who held office between the fifteenth and the twentieth century, the Turks have on 105 occasions driven Patriarchs from their throne; there have been 27 abdications, often involuntary; 6 Patriarchs have suffered violent deaths by hanging, poisoning or drowning; and only 21 have died natural deaths while in office.' In the seventy-five years between 1625 and 1700 there were fifty Patriarchs: an average of eighteen months each."[18] It is from this historic perspective that one must evaluate the justifiable protests against the present Turkish government in behalf of Ecumenical Patriarch Athenagoras I.

Periodic protests have been echoed in recent years by Pope Paul VI, Archbishop Iakovos, Dr. R. H. Edwin Espy, General Secretary of the National Council of Churches, and others over the possible expulsion of the Patriarchate and the distressing acts of unfriendliness shown by the government.[19] Much of the government's attitude supposedly reflects sympathy for the Turkish minority in Cyprus and the current hostile relations with Greek Cypriots. Historically, however, since the conquest of Constantinople by the Turks in the fifteenth century, the Byzantine Patriarchate has regularly undergone numerous subjections and subordinating adjustments to the reigning Turkish authorities.

Since the publication of Vatican II's Declaration on Religious Freedom, it has become almost commonplace for the churches to insist upon the dignity of persons and the rights of all minority peoples. However, among Orthodox majorities the question of religious liberty and special privileges granted by the state to the church are at times in conflict. For example, although Greece's constitution proclaims religious freedom, the prevailing Greek Orthodox Church, with its special privileges from the state, in practice considers the activities of all other faiths to be acts of proselytizing which are forbidden. We must be sympathetic to the Orthodox fear of proselytism, since they have been subject to much abuse from Islamic and Christian missionaries (Protestants and Roman Catholics), but that does not excuse them from following the fundamentally sound theological principles inherent in religious freedom. Protests in behalf of the Ecumenical Patriarch by Orthodox and non-Orthodox alike should hold equally true within Greece or wherever else Orthodoxy is in the controlling majority.

In summary, the contemporary and historic examples from the Byzantine past to the present illustrate that a harmonious

symphony has not been achieved through the centuries; either
the church or the state has tended to dominate. It is therefore
not surprising even in our day to see that church-state relationships may vary greatly in different Orthodox countries, as evidenced in the Soviet Union, Rumania, Greece, Cyprus, and
Ethiopia. The Biblical riddle and principle *Reddite Caesari,
reddite Deo* continues to ensnare and to perplex Christians.
Most Christians belong existentially neither entirely to Caesar
nor to God. Awareness of this ambiguous situation might well
mark the beginning steps out of our present puzzlement. Not
only in the East, but also in the West, Christians are called
upon to struggle creatively with the tensions between church
and state inherent in their respective societies.

Social Consciousness and the State

Related to the political factors of society are the social factors which confront the Christian church in both the East and
West. What concern is Orthodoxy showing for these social
factors? Is there any social consciousness among Eastern
churchmen? Many Western churchmen have raised the question, wondering quite frankly if there is any social awareness
in Orthodoxy. If Orthodoxy is viewed as a church shrouded in
sacramental mysticism with an eschatological orientation, the
inquiry can candidly be made, What real concern can she
possibly have for the misery, injustice, and need of people
now? Does Orthodoxy have anything comparable to a Walter
Rauschenbusch and the Social Gospel movement? Is Orthodoxy, to use a familiar cliché, so "heavenly-minded that she is
no earthly good"? Was the lack of social consciousness in
Orthodoxy's "Holy Russia" a major contributing factor to the
Bolshevik Revolution of 1917? These and countless other
queries have been seriously and earnestly raised by theologians, pastors, and laymen in the West of their counterparts
in the East.

In the stirring film *He Who Must Die,* based upon *The*

Greek Passion, a novel by Nikos Kazantzakis, or in the telling
historical novel *The Forty Days of Musa Dagh,* by Franz
Werfel, one is immediately struck by the severe restriction
and limitation placed upon Eastern Christians by their long
domination under Islamic rule. Under this long and heavy
shadow of the minaret, the silhouette of the cross has been
dimmed and with it much of the visible social concern of
Orthodoxy, for the sake of her very survival. This suppression
of outward social consciousness has negatively manifested
itself in a ghetto mentality within most Orthodox communities.
These communities have been preoccupied with their own
survival and have had time for nothing else. Incidents that
illustrate this struggle are portrayed vividly and indelibly in
these novels by Kazantzakis and Werfel. In many Orthodox
villages today this introverted state of behavior continues as a
way of life. Those of us in the West need first to show sympathy for their situation and history of cultural imprisonment
before we critically dismiss them as lacking social endeavors.
Actually, it is a wonder that Orthodoxy has survived under
such extreme and difficult turmoil.

However, on closer examination, even within these prohibi-
tive conditions of the past and present times, countless martyrs
within Orthodox communities seek to dissolve the ghetto and
penetrate in some relevant way into the secular culture of the
day. Most of these martyrs are unknown to us, but it is their
witness nevertheless that testifies to the fact that social consciousness is not alien to Orthodox theology, and is actually
an integral part of her sacramental mysticism and eschatological outlook. Nissiotis reminds us that it is Orthodoxy uniquely
which brings the significant contribution of her past history of
suffering in the world to the current ecumenical conversations.

It is this heritage of martyrdom rather than a list of social
projects which ought to command the West's attention and
respect for the East. Yet Western churchmen often hold, as did
the late Adolf von Harnack at the beginning of this ecumenical
century, disparaging views of Orthodox life and theology.[20]

Today, in the second half of the century and in spite of increased dialogue between East and West, there are still many
who tenaciously hold to Harnack's characterization of Orthodoxy as exclusively otherworldly, and who have not taken
another look at Orthodox theology and practice.

Orthodox social consciousness is vitally linked to Orthodoxy's theological understanding of the incarnation and resurrection celebrated by the Holy Eucharist. The Eucharistic
celebration is at the heart of Orthodox theology and life. This
Eucharistic practice highlights the significance and centrality
of the incarnation and resurrection for the believer, and from
these theological events he derives his social concern. This
becomes quite evident in the words of the Liturgy of Basil the
Great, specifically in the following prayer after the consecration of the elements in the Eucharist, which carries overtones
of social awareness throughout:

Have in remembrance, O Lord, this congregation here
present, and those who are absent for reasonable cause; and
have mercy upon them and upon us, according to the multitude of Thy mercies. Fill their treasuries with every good
thing; maintain their marriage bond in peace and concord;
rear the infants; guide the young; support the aged; encourage
the fainthearted. Collect the scattered and turn them from
their wandering astray, and unite them to Thy Holy Catholic
and Apostolic Church. Set at liberty those who are vexed by
unclean spirits; voyage with those who voyage; journey with
those who journey; defend the widows; protect the orphans;
free the captives; heal the sick. Have in remembrance, O God,
those who are under trial, and in the mines and in prison, and
in bitter labours, and in all affliction, distress and tribulation.

Have in remembrance, O God, all those who invoke Thy
great loving-kindness; those also who love us, and those who
hate us, and those who have enjoined us, unworthy though we
are, that we should pray for them; and all Thy people, O Lord,
our God: And upon them all pour out Thy rich mercy, grant-
ing unto all such of their petitions as are unto salvation. And
those whom we, through ignorance, or forgetfulness, or the

multitude of names, have not remembered, do Thou Thyself call to mind, O God, who knowest every man even from his mother's womb. For Thou, O Lord, art the Helper of the helpless, the Hope of the hopeless, the Saviour of the storm tossed, the Haven of the voyager, the Healer of the sick. Be Thyself all things unto all men, O Thou Who knowest every man, his petitions, his abode, and his need. Deliver, O Lord, this city and every city and land from famine, plague, earthquake, flood, fire, sword, the invasion of enemies, and from civil war.[21]

The consecration of the Eucharistic elements prior to this prayer of Basil is actually the reenacting of the incarnation and the resurrection. The basic theological understanding underlying the incarnation and resurrection for the Orthodox is the important concept of *metamorphosis:* incarnation and resurrection point to transformation and transfiguration. In acceptance of the incarnation and resurrection, the believer is given the social possibility of metamorphosis for man and for society. The concept of metamorphosis conveys a dimension of divine responsibility for the believer and the community. This in turn provides the believer with divine sanction to show social concern for his neighbor in the world, striving toward the transformation and transfiguration of his neighbor and his environment into something finer and nobler. This is precisely why the early church fathers stressed the incarnation and resurrection as theological guidelines for the believer's physical as well as spiritual goals.

The monastic communities in Orthodoxy themselves were viewed as a theological expression and foretaste of the transfigured communal society as attempted in The Acts of the Apostles (cf. Acts 4:32–33)—a community of love and concern. Monasticism seen from this social perspective was not so much a retreat from life as an advance into a nobler life. The monks were the social army of the church, establishing inlets of hope and social welfare in the world, anticipating the final end and renewal of all life when the Kingdom of God shall be finally realized. Hence, the monks combined Ortho-

doxy's eschatological bent with a current concern for the
material needs of people. Monasteries were dedicated to physical as well as spiritual welfare.[22] As a social army of protest,
the monks refused to submit to the secular pressures of their
day because of their anticipation of the *eschaton*. This eschatological hope within Orthodoxy can therefore be interpreted
prophetically as well as in otherworldly terms.

Later, under the secular reforms of Peter the Great, monastic
social effectiveness was largely reduced; the monks and the
church were made subservient to the state. (It should be remembered that the Russian Orthodox Church is the largest
in Orthodoxy and at the time of Peter's reign the only significant church not under Islamic jurisdiction.) Peter's state-
oriented reforms came as a blow to the Russian Church's
vitality. Today, Peter's political philosophy is continued by the
Soviet State, thus restricting the expression of social consciousness by the church. The ambiguous church-state relationship
characteristic of Orthodoxy is perhaps the greatest single factor in suppressing Orthodox social consciousness.

Even prior to the peak of Islamic rule, Hellenic and Slavic
Orthodoxy were already subject to a circumscribed role in
society due to the Byzantine structure of the state. In reality,
the symphonic or harmonious Byzantine doctrine of the church
and state revealed, more often than not, the subservience of
the church to the state, thus preventing the church from witnessing in all areas of life and culture. As a result, the church
was permitted to administer in areas pertaining to heaven
while the state administered in areas pertaining to earth.
Obviously, such a division of human society is impossible; it
points to a false fragmentation of human life and needs.
Nevertheless, this view was espoused, and as a consequence
put the church on the periphery of irrelevance. With the
exception primarily of the monastic movement, which experienced some independence and self-sufficiency from the state
in order to carry out a total ministry, Byzantine church life
was forced to conceal its social concern.

The communal emphasis, typified at the height of monastic life, continues to prevail in contemporary Orthodox life. Even today, social consciousness in Orthodoxy is nurtured mainly in a communal context. Orthodox followers tend to voice their social concern as a community rather than as individuals.[23] This communal type of social action is directly related to the Orthodox understanding of the church as a fusion of individuals, freely operating in love for the sake of the body of Christ which is his humanity. The stress upon togetherness, wholeness, and community (better known as *sobornost'*) adds a valuable dimension to social activity not often seen in the West. The Orthodox design to relate the individual to the community and the community to the individual is perhaps a greater and more enduring act of charity than simply some isolated act of kindness. This family quality of Orthodox social consciousness embraces the individual and sincerely invites him to become a part of the whole without destroying his own individuality. While this family approach gives a quality of warmth especially needed in a depersonalized age of automation, weakness can be found in its customary limit along ethnic and national lines. Orthodoxy must be constantly challenged to cross ethnic barriers. Perhaps the greatest contribution of the Orthodox churches in America will lie in this direction, where they are being forced to break from their ethnic structures and accept the pluralistic cultural frame of America.

As Orthodoxy is able to overcome these nationalistic inclinations, her potentiality for social witness will increase in today's ecumenical climate. The youth of Orthodoxy in particular are seeking the spirit of social consciousness as they restudy their church's history, especially the fathers of the faith who sought to humanize Byzantine life, which was based at that time upon slavery and despotism. John Chrysostom, no less than Rauschenbusch, sounded the note of social concern, and is regarded by many in both the East and the West as the earliest apostle of social justice. In those difficult days, the Byzantine Church reminded people of the meaning of mercy and love by feeding the poor, establishing hospitals, lodging, and other forms of social service.

Continuing in that same Byzantine spirit of social charity, the Greek Orthodox Church today has in the dioceses of Greece centers of philanthropic activity. "Not only has the Church issued encyclicals expressive of her concern for social justice, but each bishop has a treasury of 'Funds for the Poor,' and maintains several welfare institutions. There are more than 140 orphanages, old-age homes, nurseries, sanatoriums, clinics, hospitals, schools for retarded children, and other philanthropic establishments, which are maintained directly by the dioceses. For example, the diocese of Dimitrias with 124 parishes maintains twelve charitable institutions. The diocese of Mesenia with a population of perhaps 100,000 supports fourteen philanthropic establishments. The diocese of Lesbos with sixty parishes supports twelve welfare institutions."[24] These examples illustrate well the presence of *philanthrōpia*, the ethics of *agapē* and social consciousness, which is characteristic of the Byzantine heritage.

Hope also emerges from the Brotherhoods of Zoë and Sotir which attempt to educate the illiterate, to preach, teach, and publish theological works to stimulate renewal and dialogue between church and culture. The Ephesos, a fellowship of theologians, is an attempt to achieve a more intensive dialogue and confrontation of the church with secular life. The Brotherhood of the Paraclete, founded more recently, is another expanding group of socially conscious churchmen who make their center in Piraeus, Greece. Somewhat like the worker-priest movement in France, these parish priests witness among the laboring class districts of Piraeus. In a unique way they combine monastic life, social concern, and an evangelical outreach toward the lower income groups.

In short, Orthodox churchmen are showing increased vigor in our day toward reasserting Orthodoxy's historic social consciousness, which has been and continues to be subject to harassment, disappointment, and martyrdom.

Part Three

SEARCH FOR SPIRITUAL RENEWAL

Chapter VIII

Easter and the Eucharistic Worship

There is no finer introduction for a Protestant to the "Candle-light Kingdom" of Eastern Christians than through its celebration of Easter and the Eucharist. Orthodox theology can be summed up in these two significant happenings—Easter and the Eucharist—which are so integrally bound together in Orthodox worship. The dramatization of these events in worship has priority over their verbalization in theological dogmas. This is in keeping with the ancient recognition that the Christian church is primarily a worshiping community. This sentiment is expressed well by the traditional adage *Lex orandi lex est credendi.* Prayer and worship have precedent over doctrine and discipline in the fellowship of the Christian community. Emphasis on worship is most evident in the Eastern tradition. To know Orthodoxy, the Westerner must enter into the cosmic strangeness of her sanctuary. Herein is preserved the life and thought, as well as the spirit and will, of Orthodox believers through the centuries.

There are many variant liturgies in the East, but the tradition of worship in Eastern Orthodoxy is basically one. This will be the viewpoint assumed in this chapter's discussion. According to Father Paul Verghese, the worshiping tradition of the East "has a pluriformity intrinsic to it. Many both within and outside that tradition are often unaware of this fact. The Byzantine form of the Orthodox tradition is the one best known in the West. But liturgical scholars know that before the development of this tradition there existed a Jerusalemite, an Antiochian, and an Alexandrian liturgical tradition. Both the Western liturgical tradition and the Byzantine are essentially derived from this earlier Asian-African tradition. Today the Orthodox liturgical tradition may be said to exist in at least six slightly different forms: the Western Syrian, the Eastern Syrian, the Egyptian, the Ethiopian, the Byzantine, and the Armenian. Admittedly there exists such a great measure of 'unanimity' between these six traditions, that they are better called subtraditions of one single tradition."[1]

A plausible hypothesis has been suggested "that the word 'Orthodoxy' in the Eastern use means primarily not 'right opinion' (as it is usually interpreted in the West), but rather 'right glory,' i.e., precisely, right worship."[2] Our concern in this chapter will be with the implications for the West of "right worship" in Orthodoxy. We will first examine an Easter service as seen through Protestant eyes, followed by a discussion on the centrality of the Eucharist, and finally we will consider whether a division need exist between a liturgical and a Biblical theology.

Easter in the Eastern Tradition

Orthodox observance of Easter was an unforgettable experience. As early as ten o'clock on Saturday evening, a large crowd had gathered in St. Sergius Russian Orthodox Church, a former German Lutheran Church sold to Russian immigrants who flocked to Paris following the Russian revolution. Almost all were standing as is the practice in traditional Orthodox services (though seats are provided in most Orthodox churches today in America), and a fabricated tomb of Jesus, draped in black and decked with flowers, was in the center of the church's interior. The atmosphere was subdued with anticipation as the choir sang softly in the background and brief prayers were given by the priests. Gradually, as midnight approached, the music and prayers quickened their pace; then in that weighty moment following midnight, the bishop appeared from behind the iconostasis (the screen of icons), holding a candle, and announced to all, *"Christos voskres"* ("Christ is risen!"). *"Voistinno voskres"* ("He is risen indeed!"), replied the enthused congregation which overflowed into the courtyard of St. Sergius. From the bishop's flame, the entire congregation lighted their individual candles announcing the new day.

The bishop then led the congregation in candlelight procession out of the sanctuary and encircled the church. When they returned, the gospel of the resurrection was repeated in five languages—Slavonic, Greek, French, German, and English—witnessing to the catholicity of the good news. Again the bishop proclaimed, "Christ is risen!" and the cry was returned by the people, "He is risen indeed!" Then the royal gates of the iconostasis were flung open to reveal a splendor of innumerable lights, typifying the glory of the empty tomb.

This dramatic service concluded with the celebration of the Eucharist followed by the traditional Easter breakfast, which lasted until five o'clock in the morning. The worshipers then retired to their homes for rest until Sunday afternoon when a second, but shorter, worship service was held at the Orthodox cemetery at Sainte-Geneviève-des-Bois outside of Paris. The afternoon service stressed the joy of Christ's resurrection for deceased loved ones. The service took place in a picturesque chapel on the grounds, with the liturgy chanted and sung in a spirited and joyful manner.

The priest ended the service by leading the congregation out of the chapel, his incense burner in hand. He was followed by two young persons carrying banners of the church, a distinguished layman of the congregation carrying the Easter cake with a single candle in the center, several individuals carrying icons of Christ, and the chapel choir. Singing along the way, the priest guided the procession through the cemetery, stopping often at the graves where family members stood by in memory of their departed loved ones. The priest greeted

each group with his proclamation, "He is risen!" and they
replied with the same happy assurance, "Indeed, he is risen!"
More than once the words of Scripture came to mind: "O
death, where is thy victory? O death, where is thy sting?"
(I Cor. 15:55). The answer to these questions was dramatically and vividly given at that moment even more eloquently
than in a sermon. Protestants as well as Roman Catholics certainly rejoice with the Orthodox in their enthusiasm for the
good news of Christ's resurrection. At the conclusion of the
day, we enjoyed together an agape feast with traditional
Orthodox Easter foods (*Pascha, Kulich,* and colored eggs).

The Easter liturgy itself must be experienced and studied
in order to grasp its mission and beauty. Schmemann discusses
in great detail the problem of the *Ordo* and the *Typicon*
(manual of worship.) By *Ordo* he means the basic structure
of worship underlying and enshrined in the *Typicon*. Schmemann confesses on behalf of the Orthodox that "worship
has ceased to be understood in its own real content, which
is to be the expression, creation, and fulfilment of the Church.
The overwhelming majority of Orthodox people have no
interest in the meaning of worship. It is accepted and experienced in mystical and aesthetic but never 'logical' categories.
It moves the soul of the believer by its sacredness, by its
mysteriousness, by its 'otherworldliness.' And everything that
happens to fall within its orbit becomes overgrown with complicated symbolic explanations. It is characteristic that in this
symbolism there is no symbolism of the Church. Thus, people
love to explain the Divine Liturgy as the depiction of the life
of Christ. But who explains it as the expression of the life of
the Church, as the action by which she is externally realized?"[3]
Schmemann is concerned by the mistaken perspective of many
Orthodox believers who subordinate the church to the worship
experience and thereby fail to see that worship is primarily a
function of the church. Worship is not an end in itself, for this
would degenerate Christianity into a saving cult instead of a
saving faith with a commission to witness in the world. Also,

if the liturgy is only in the chancel and not in the pews, it is only a book of suggestions at the disposal of the minister. A liturgy must be in the hands (or better, in the hearts) of the people; otherwise, it is only a source book for the clergy.

The liturgical worship of Orthodoxy aspires to fulfill a vision of heaven on earth. The church herself is an island of heaven upon the earth. Therefore the church through her physical structure and through the voice of her liturgy "has attempted by every element of material splendor and beauty to form the earthly Liturgy as an ikon of the celestial Liturgy. Whether in great cathedral or in peasant church the prayerful attitude, the clouds of incense, the mystery and awe, have all lent an overwhelming impression of the supernatural. This experience so often remarked upon by Westerners attending the Eastern Liturgy has formed the Christians of the East much more than consideration of doctrine and discipline. These good people have been so formed in the Divine Liturgy that in the darkest periods of history whether under Muslim, Tartar, or Commissar it has been the Divine Liturgy that inspired and gave them hope—it is the most constant expression of Orthodox belief."[4] It is therefore very meaningful to catch a glimpse of the worshipers during the service. Their lives and those of their ancestors represent a history of blood, tears, and hardships in which the liturgy has been an unlimited supply of strength in its concrete symbolism.

Before continuing, let us examine briefly the conflicting dates of Easter in the East and in the West. Fixing the date of Easter was a difficult problem for the early church. The First Ecumenical Council of Nicaea (in A.D. 325) proposed that the Festival of the Resurrection be celebrated on the Sunday following the first full moon of spring. In order to calculate the date of Easter according to the decision of Nicaea, the beginning of spring must be determined. At the time of the Council of Nicaea, spring began on the twenty-first of March. But the Julian calendar, which was then in use, had inaccuracies which during the course of time separated the twenty-first of March from the real beginning of spring. By 1582 there was already a discrepancy of ten days, for the spring equinox that year really occurred on the eleventh of March. Pope Gregory XIII therefore introduced a reform of the Julian calendar, the so-called "Gregorian reform." He decided that the year 1582 should be shortened by ten days, and in order to avoid further discrepancies he decreed that in the future there should be ninety-seven leap years every four hundred years (instead of one hundred leap years as formerly.)[5] The Eastern churches beyond the sphere of Roman influence retained the Julian calendar. The problem is not confined to Easter; it covers the whole period from Lent to Pentecost. In today's ecumenical climate, there is a strong desire on the part of all the churches to resolve the differences, extending the work of the Universal Christian Council for Life and Work (1932) and the investigations of the League of Nations in their efforts of three decades earlier. Orthodox, Protestants, and Roman Catholics are showing a willingness today for a common date for Easter, "the Queen of Feasts," for the West as well as for the East.

Centrality of the Eucharistic Worship

The Easter liturgy signifies not only the eschatological but also the Eucharistic heart of Orthodox worship. The Spirit-filled moment of the liturgy is seen in the celebration of the Holy Eucharist, where the worshiper is able to eat and drink in the presence of his Lord. Everything in the liturgy refers to the incarnation, and everything in turn leads to the Lord. "The liturgy integrates the most elementary actions of life: drinking, eating, washing, speaking, acting, communicating, living—and restores to them their meaning and their true destiny: to be parts of the cosmic Temple of God's Glory."[6] The Holy Eucharist is a visible sign of our sacramental universe.

Orthodoxy believes in the total consecration of matter. "The world was created as the 'matter,' the material of one all-embracing eucharist, and man was created as the priest of this

cosmic sacrament."[7] According to Father Alexander Schmemann, "Men understand all this instinctively if not rationally.
Centuries of secularism have failed to transform eating into
something strictly utilitarian. Food is still treated with reverence. A meal is still a rite—the last 'natural sacrament' of
family and friendship, of life that is more than 'eating' and
'drinking.' To eat is still something more than to maintain
bodily functions. People may not understand what that 'something more' is, but they nonetheless desire to celebrate it. They
are still hungry and thirsty for sacramental life."[8] Thus for the
Orthodox, man's situation today may be characterized as one
of forsakenness toward the sacramental nature of life, living
a "noneucharistic life in a noneucharistic world."[9] The over-
coming of man's fallen state depends on a transformation of
his perspective to see the world once again in its sacramental
dimension.

The Eucharist is a sacrament of cosmic remembrance. In
the liturgy, the whole sacrificial life of Christ is recalled from
Bethlehem to Pentecost: divided into three parts—the liturgy
of preparation, the liturgy of the catechumens, and the climac-
tic liturgy of the faithful in which the elements are partaken
by the believers. The Eucharist represents a continual intercession on the part of Jesus to the Father through the invocation of the Holy Spirit (the Epiclesis).[10] The act of intercession
is an act of remembrance in love. "God remembers us and his
remembrance, his love is the foundation of the world. In
Christ, we *remember*. We become again beings open to love,
and we *remember*. The Church in its separation from 'this
world,' on its journey to heaven *remembers* the world, remembers all men, remembers the whole of creation, takes it in
love to God. The Eucharist is the sacrament of cosmic remembrance: it is indeed a restoration of love as the very life
of the world."[11]

The Eucharist as cosmic remembrance is actually a *representation*, a making present again of Christ's redeeming life
and work. This does not mean a repetition of the Last Supper

and Calvary (this is not possible from an Eastern viewpoint),
but rather that the Eucharistic event involves more than historic comprehension as a past event; it is cosmic and even
contemporaneous in dimension. Mystically, the Eucharist still
"continues and is open to new generations of believers, in the
unbroken unity of the one Body of Christ which is the Church.
The sacrifice of Christ was universal and all-inclusive. At
every celebration believers are, as it were, taken back to the
Upper Room, precisely at the moment of the Last Supper. It
is to say that essentially every celebration is the Last Supper
itself. The mystery (i.e., the 'sacrament') is one and ever the
same, even as the sacrifice is one, and the table ever one.
Christ Jesus is *present*, both as the Minister of the Sacrament,
and as the Victim—'who offers and is offered.' He is the ultimate and perennial Minister of the Church, the true High-
Priest of the New Testament, 'in His blood.' This 'sacramental
realism' explains that august place which is given to the Sacrament in the life of the Church. It is the spring and the root of
her spiritual existence."[12] This is the mystical context of realism
in which the Orthodox celebrate the Eucharist in contrast to
the formalized traditional understanding of transubstantiation
found in the Roman Church.

The centrality of the Eucharist in Eastern worship enables
the non-Orthodox to gain deeper appreciation of the Christian
church as a Eucharistic community.[13] From the viewpoint of
the community, the Eucharist is an act of thanksgiving. In this
sense, the Eucharist is an anaphora, the consecration or lifting
up of our offerings and, above all, of ourselves. As an act of
remembrance and thanksgiving, the Eucharist is what actually
binds the community together in doxology to the Father, Son,
and Spirit. The community of believers and the community
within the Godhead are thereby united through participation
in the sacramental mystery (*mystērion*) of the Eucharist.[14]
Thus Eastern worship is a communal matter, both in its relation to man and to God, Eucharistically and eschatologically
embracing in its mysterious way the past, present, and future

in God's cosmos. Thereby the liturgy encourages the community of believers to extend themselves mystically beyond time and space to the glories and promises of the world to come.

In the Eucharistic community the other sacraments of Baptism, Chrismation (confirmation), penance, anointing of the sick (Holy Unction), holy orders, and marriage are all related and find their unity in the Eucharist. "The Eucharist is the *mystērion* par excellence, which is more than merely nourishment for the Body of Christ. It is, in fact, the *raison d'etre* of the Body of Christ in the world of space and time. All 'sacraments' are completed by the Eucharist."[15] The prominence of the Eucharist as the unifying sacrament is undisputed among Eastern Christians. However, the actual number of sacraments is a disputed question among them. Some Orthodox consider the question to be open-ended, while others fix the number at seven, taking their clue from the Second Council of Lyons (1274) which fixed that number. It is equally clear that there has been no conciliar decree officially recognized by the Orthodox which fixes the number at seven or specifies which seven. It is this degree of openness along with the whole sacramental approach toward life which promises fruitful opportunity for further discussion between Protestants and Orthodox.

The present comments on the centrality of the Eucharistic worship would be incomplete without mentioning the question of intercommunion between Orthodox and non-Orthodox. There is a great deal of literature on the subject, but the actual experience of intercommunion by Orthodox with either Roman Catholics or Protestants is still distant. There have been instances of intercommunion on isolated occasions when necessity warranted it and the charity of churchmen in the respective traditions have made it possible. This is known as "economic intercommunion" by the Orthodox as opposed to "ordinary intercommunion." The latter "is a relationship established between two Churches, more or less explicitly with a view to fuller unity, whereas economic intercommunion is concerned

primarily with individuals and their specific pastoral needs.
Economic intercommunion occurs when a particular person—
desiring the sacraments and cut off from the ministrations of
his own Church is allowed by way of hospitality to receive the
Holy Gifts at the altar of another Church. According to Orthodox theology, however, such an act of 'economic' admission to
the sacraments is not to be interpreted as establishing a relationship of intercommunion between the two Churches as
such. It is not a question of inter-Church relations, of steps
towards reunion, but simply of an individual Christian believer
and his salvation."[16] Each case is decided individually and
does not set any precedent for future acts of intercommunion.

The Christian church as a Eucharistic community uniting
East and West does not as yet exist. The climate in these post-
Vatican II years is encouraging, but false optimism is to be
avoided. Cardinal Lercaro, Archbishop of Bologna, has rightly
stated:

> *Communicatio in sacris* involves the depths of the mystery
> of the Unity of the Church, and cannot be practiced lightly.
> Still less can it become a camouflaged form of Proselytism.
> A *sine qua non* condition, if it is not to be ecumenically harm-
> ful, is that it is accepted consciously and sincerely by the two
> groups. It can never be an individual affair, but necessarily
> commits the responsible leaders of the two Churches. In order
> to be a means of rapprochement, leading to full communion
> between ourselves and our Eastern brethren, it has to be ex-
> plicitly agreed upon by the Catholic bishops and the Orthodox
> bishops. We recognize in these latter the essential marks of the
> true Church. This it is which allows us to propose to them the
> *communicatio,* but we are not in any way able to impose it
> upon them nor practice it against their will. That would be to
> act in a way diametrically opposed to the spirit which *De
> Oecumenismo* wishes to encourage: that is, respect for the
> non-Catholic Churches as Churches. To practice the *com-
> municatio* against their will or without their consent would be
> to disregard their ecclesial character.[17]

Admittedly, it is difficult for many Protestants to appreciate
the depth of understanding evident in Cardinal Lercaro's
statement. Protestants theologically stand for word and sacrament, but in practice tend to devaluate the sacraments for the
word. Thus a Protestant experiencing an Orthodox service may
assume the antidoron, the blessed bread signifying the New
Testament agape which is distributed at the end of the service
to Orthodox and non-Orthodox alike, only a short step from
actual participation in the elements of the Eucharist prepared
for the Orthodox faithful during the liturgy. However, from
the Orthodox standpoint, the issue goes far deeper and questions the validity of the Protestant ordained ministry in a way
in which it does not with the Roman priesthood.

For some Orthodox, in fact, the possibility of intercommunion with Roman Catholics in principle is conceivable,
since the two traditions mutually recognize each other's orders
and sacraments as being based on apostolic succession. The
only obstacles these Orthodox (who are a very small minority)
see between themselves and Roman Catholics are disciplinary
and not doctrinal in nature.[18] The majority within Orthodoxy,
however, believe that intercommunion with both Protestants
and Roman Catholics can come only after long and tedious
dialogue in which differences are overcome and resolved.
Disciplinary issues and matters of canonical jurisdiction also
have their doctrinal side, and therefore cannot be easily dismissed. To dismiss these differences or to rationalize them for
most Orthodox would undermine the centrality and authenticity of the Eucharistic worship. For the Orthodox, the Eucharist is not a pragmatic tool for seeking unity but the fruit
of unity following the restoration of fellowship among the
churches.

The Orthodox stand may appear stubborn to the non-Orthodox and insulting to Protestants. Those who have been involved in the ecumenical work of this century, among both
Orthodox and Protestants, know how theologically embar-

rassing and even tragic the situation can be. But if the Eucharist is to be regarded so highly by the Orthodox as the sacrament of unity and the moment of truth, Protestants should support their Eastern brethren, not cheapen that which symbolizes and nourishes their devotion.

According to Orthodox theologian N. A. Nissiotis, the "liturgy signifies our belonging together organically and spiritually to the one Ecclesia; before and after the Holy Communion, this fact must be concretely manifested and maintained. A Roman Catholic cannot communicate and then 'return' to his previous attitude regarding those with whom he communicated as 'separated' brethren. The Reformed cannot return after the communion to his own tradition, and still regard it as separated from the Eastern Church and willingly act as one alienated from the Eastern tradition in which he shared the body and blood of the One Body of Christ in its pre-existing unity, as the Orthodox believe they have kept it. On the other hand, following the Orthodox understanding of communion we could not accept a unilateral intercommunion, i.e., individuals of other Churches participating in the Orthodox Eucharist while the Orthodox are not yet able to participate in their Eucharist. An intercommunion implies full mutual communion."[19] Until this full mutual communion among the churches is known, both the East and the West must face the bitterness of separation in prayerful intercession for one another.

Liturgical or Biblical Theology?

In our discussion thus far, we have seen the liturgical emphasis focused upon the sacrament of the Holy Eucharist in Eastern worship. This raises many serious questions for the Protestant who places his emphasis upon the preached word in his worship experience. Protestant worship is largely oriented between two focuses—the voice of the preacher and the ear of the listener. Orthodoxy in its liturgical practice is highly sensual and sacramental. Are these two ways of worship incompatible? The Eastern Christian views the Protestant West as antiliturgical and subsequently antisacramental.[20] The Protestant sees the Orthodox worshiper as Biblically illiterate and his liturgy in competition with the Scriptures. The stereotyped images that each holds of the other make dialogue nearly impossible. Is there a way out of this impasse?

On closer study, both the Orthodox and non-Orthodox must mutually discover that a liturgical and sacramental theology is Biblical, and that a Biblical theology is also liturgical and sacramental. From the Eastern standpoint, the words of the liturgy pointing toward the Eucharist are derived from Scripture. It is only a superficial survey which leads a Protestant to think that the liturgy and Scripture are widely separated. Liturgy and the Bible are entirely fused into one for the Orthodox. One Orthodox theological student indicated, "We have more of the Bible read in our services than you have in yours." His statement at first is surprising, but it is true. The use of Scripture in the Orthodox liturgy reproduces the Bible for the present as living tradition. The liturgy actually unites the written Word with the unwritten life of the Christian church. Furthermore, the unity of liturgy and Scripture chanted by the Orthodox priest helps the believers to see Christ as the High Priest who intercedes in their behalf.

In a research study on the Byzantine liturgies of St. John Chrysostom, St. Basil, and the Presanctified (the liturgies best known in the West) as well as the sacramental services of Baptism, Chrismation, Holy Unction, and Matrimony, a clear relationship was found between these services of worship and their dependence upon Scripture. Approximately 25 percent of these services consist of almost direct Biblical material. The content of the liturgy that alludes to Scripture is even greater.[21] The study also revealed that the liturgical authors used both Testaments but slightly favored the Old over the New. The Hebrew influence inherent in Orthodox worship would be a fruitful avenue for further investigation, especially in the light

of the increasing Christian-Jewish dialogue. The use of the
book of The Psalms in the liturgies exceeds by far the other
books of the Bible. This fact is not only revealing for purposes
of ecumenical exchange, but even more it indicates that a
theological and liturgical study of the soteriological nature of
The Psalms is needed in our rapidly developing ecumenical
climate.

The Gospel According to Matthew comes second, and the
book of Genesis is third in number of appearances in the three
basic Byzantine liturgies. In the Old Testament, Genesis is
followed by Isaiah, Exodus, and the deuterocanonical books
(Apocrypha)—the Wisdom of Solomon and Judith. In the
New Testament, Matthew is followed by the Gospel of Luke,
I Corinthians, Romans, and the Gospel of John in that order.
The letter to the Hebrews also enjoys wide representation in
the liturgies, indicating that the liturgical authors had considerable knowledge of the recognized Scriptures of that day.

In short, there is adequate evidence that the liturgical
writers were dependent upon Biblical materials. It would be
a false dichotomy to pit liturgy vs. Scripture in voicing support
for one tradition against another. Both Orthodoxy and Protestantism are committed to a Biblical basis in their understanding of worship as doxology. For the primary aim of a Biblical
liturgy, whether in the East or in the West, is to praise and
glorify the Triune God in thanksgiving. "Worship is thus the
realization of grace and freedom. Joy is its constitutive mark.
Salvation means freedom to worship. And worship is life, here
as well as in the world to come. This authentic tone of freedom, grace, and joy must find expression in our worship, for
these are the qualities of true human existence. Other qualities
which will meet the needs of man, modern or ancient, will also
be created in the worshipping community, only when worship
finds its true orientation."[22]

A true orientation is one that does not assign priority to
man's psychological and sociological needs, but rather redis-
covers his current restlessness as residing in his eschatological

nature which longs for refreshment and repose. Authentic worship seeks to nurture man's eschatological being; that is, it addresses itself to man's anticipatory nature, removing his fear and anxiety for tomorrow with praise, thanksgiving, and confidence in his Creator. Man has never wanted to live in a flat world; he is a cosmic being. Worship as an eschatological exercise in doxology speaks to the cosmic dimensions of man. An emerging East-West theology will seek to create a Biblical and Eucharistic liturgy that will bear faithful witness to the liturgical authors of the past, directing the worshiper to give "right glory" to God and thereby fulfill his human destiny.

There is probably no greater task for theologians in the East and the West than to study seriously the rich diversity found in their existing liturgies and to anticipate creatively in the spirit of their church fathers new models for a living liturgy.[23] A living liturgy (or liturgies) is sought which will unite Christians, but which will at the same time avoid a stale uniformity for the Christians of tomorrow.

The gifts of freedom, grace, and joy from God are centered in the Eucharist, a common meal meant to unite all his followers. Our respective liturgies of the Eucharist, heavily weighted with theological overtones, have divided us from experiencing a common meal. Perhaps it is not our liturgies, saturated in the Biblical revelation, which need to be transformed, but rather our theological biases with their accompanying attitudes of suspicion which must come under God's judgment. Liturgies and theological interpretations are inseparably joined together. It would be naïve to think that theology alone has corrupted the liturgies and turned them into vehicles of disunity. Ecumenical awareness has taught us that all aspects of Christian life and worship are relational and therefore connective. We live in the midst of a theological stream of grayness; it is difficult to isolate our problems without involving an entire set of causes and effects. No small factor is the idolatrous attitudes which we bring to each other's liturgies, coated in theological jargon and making a mockery

out of both our liturgies and our respective traditions. Hope
lies in increased self-awareness as members of the body of
Christ who come to celebrate his sacrifice and his victory in
our behalf.

The Eucharist is the act in which the church heightens her
understanding and awareness of herself. In the midst of our
separateness, let us come seeking greater self-awareness and
thereby atone for our divisions before the Eucharist celebrated
in our several traditions. Hope lies in the authenticity of our
spirit of penance. Let us not cheapen the Eucharist into a mere
means to a noble end. From a pragmatic viewpoint, admittedly, this is disheartening. We are impatient for action. The
tension between continuity with the past and the demand for
immediate change in the present is too much for many to bear.
Some have opted for the past and others for the present. From
the perspective of ecumenical realism, instant unity is shallow.
Our hope lies in the future, and our future has already begun
in our current involvements with each other under the specter
of our disunity.

The Eucharistic prayer in the Liturgy of St. Basil should
continue to challenge not only the Christians of the East but
of the West as well:

May thou unite us all, as many as are partakers in the one
bread and cup, one with another, in the participation of the
one Holy Spirit: to suffer no one of us to partake of the holy
body and blood of thy Christ unto judgment or unto condem-
nation; but that thereby we may find mercy and grace together
with all the saints which have been well-pleasing unto thee
since the world began, our forefathers and fathers, Patriarchs,
Prophets, Apostles, Preachers, Gospellers, Martyrs, Confessors,
Doctors, and with all the spirits of the just in faith made
perfect.[24]

Easter and the Eucharistic worship are thus triumphant
notes of Christian faith for all believers. The East no less than

the West testifies to this fact in their contrasting ways of worship. The aim of our discussion has been to highlight the significance of these momentous events and to underline the shared responsibility which falls upon us all to be united in our praise, thanksgiving, and glory to God in the name of the Father, Son, and Holy Spirit.

Chapter IX

The Art and Mission
of the Icon

A discussion of Easter and the Eucharist in Eastern worship would be incomplete without mention of the visual dimension supplied by the presence of icons. The icon and the liturgy are mutually interdependent. Icons are an expression of liturgical art. This is most significantly seen in the Byzantine Orthodox churches. In these churches icons are witnesses to the reality of the incarnation, pointing the believer to the goal of his pilgrimage celebrated in the events of Easter and the Eucharist. The Eucharistic liturgy provides the context and gives meaning to the icon as liturgical art.

Icon as Liturgical Art

The numerous icons displayed in an Orthodox sanctuary are more than attractive pieces of art. The icon is not simply a decorative item as a Westerner might suppose; an icon is not even considered religious art. "What we tend to call a work of religious art is a work with a religious theme. If it is of the Christian tradition that we are speaking, then a work of religious art is a work which presents to our view scenes drawn from the Scriptures or from the lives of the saints or from some other recognized source. Because an icon also presents such a subject, we classify it too as religious, as we do a picture of the holy family by Raphael or of the crucifixion by Matisse. In so doing, we forget that what determines the nature of a work of art is not so much its subject as its form; and that while a work of art may be called religious because its subject is drawn from the storehouse of scriptural text or sacred legend, it cannot be called an icon unless it derives from *spiritual vision,* spiritual understanding, and is fused (though not confused) with this spiritual content."[1] In short, an icon is a link between the eternal and the temporal, serving as an image of the divine world even to the extent that it partakes in the spiritual energy of what it portrays, thereby aiding the worshiper as a bridge or signpost for his own pilgimage through this earthly life. For the Eastern worshiper, an icon is a form of sacramental presence and therefore a channel of grace in the growth and nurture of the Christian life.

The role of the icon in the life of the Orthodox believer is not to be minimized. The icons in his home are an extension of the presence of the liturgical mystery which he experiences in church. The icon serves as an integrative element in the worshiper's entire style of life. "This is a vital point, for it is impossible to understand an icon apart from this integration. In the homes of the faithful the icon is placed high up, at the focal point of the room, so that one's view is directed towards the one thing necessary. In prayerful contemplation the gaze passes through the icon, as it were, to come to rest at the living content it expresses. Through its liturgical function (synthesis of sense and presence), the icon consecrates the profane, transforming a neutral dwelling-place into a 'domestic church,' and the life of the faithful into a prayer-life of interior and unceasing liturgy."[2] Thus the usual practice on entering an Orthodox home is for the visitor (if he is Orthodox) to bow before the icon as before the sight of God; and then to greet the master of the house. "One begins by honouring God; the honours paid to men come after that. As the focal point, and never a mere decoration, an icon centers the whole interior on the radiating influence of the beyond, which alone is abso-

lute."[3] Whether at home or in the church, the icon is not only
a reminder but a presence of the unceasing life promised the
worshiper in the grace of God.

Because the icon is a sacramental channel of grace it is
distinguished from a picture or a portrait with a religious
theme or subject. The icon participates in the divine reality
and energy, for without this participation it would be truly
flat, lifeless, and empty of any spiritual vision. The icon artist
is the medium through which the eschatological reality receives its temporal expression. The image or reality envisioned
is greater than the producer or the materials which have gone
into the production of the icon. The spiritual vision is supreme
and radiates the sacramental presence of grace. Ultimately
this cannot be explained; it can only be experienced. The icon
is an extension of the liturgical mystery witnessed in the
Eucharist. By this sacramental character, an icon exists truly
and independently of the artist and the spectator, directing
both to the transcendent reality to which it witnesses. "The
artist effaces himself behind a tradition, the work of art
becomes the milieu of a theophany before which it is impossible to remain a mere spectator, and man falls prostrate in an
act of adoration and prayer."[4] Only as a Protestant appreciates
this perspective will he be able adequately to evaluate theologically the function of the icon.

The proper context for the icon is liturgical and eschatological. Without this context, the spiritual vision depicted in
the icon cannot be nurtured and sustained. "Divorced from
this whole, hung in a frame upon a wall, and looked at as an
individual aesthetic object, it is divorced from the context in
which it can function as an icon. It may then be an attractive
piece of decoration, but as an icon it ceases to exist. For as an
icon it can only exist within the particular framework of belief
and worship to which it belongs. An icon divorced from this
framework ceases to be an icon. An icon divorced from a place
and act of worship is a contradiction in terms."[5] Unfortunately,

some practices among the theologically ignorant in Orthodoxy distort the function of the icon and remove it from the liturgical setting. Such practices should be noted and corrected, but to dismiss the use of icons because of their occasional misuse would be too harsh a judgment. What church tradition is free from abuse of its sacred trust and heritage?

The icon, like the Eucharist, participates in the divine reality. The Eucharist may be considered the image or icon of Christ; the icons in the church (and at home) are images of the Eucharist, leading the mind to the Eucharist, to the heart of the Christian mystery. "For the icon testifies to the basic realities of the Christian faith—to the reality of the divine penetration of the human and natural world, and to the reality of that sanctification which results from this. And as these two basic realities also contain and imply a whole cosmology, the icon also testifies to the Christian scheme of the universe, to the Christian world-picture."[6] Such a depicted cosmology is a valuable eschatological reminder to Christians living in a shrinking world that their separate worlds, East and West, are becoming an anachronistic designation in today's technopolis. All humanity stands under the Creator's judgment and mercy. Only a Biblical cosmology with an eschatological thrust will be suitable for tomorrow's cosmopolis; anything less is provincial theologizing.

The world of icons is not an imitation of the natural world; rather, it is an eschatological view of man and society as they ought to be. The icon "does not enter into competition with the unattainable perfection of the world, as classical art, for instance, so often tries to do; nor does it aspire, again as classical art so often does aspire, to a serenity in terms of this world— an aspiration which, because of its impossibility, results in a falsifying idealism. On the contrary, the icon seeks to express a structure of ideas. It seeks to convey to us a picture of the divine world order—that is, a picture of how things are in their true state, or in 'the eyes of God,' and not as they appear to us from our limited points of view."[7] From such a vantage point, there is a timelessness about the icons as there is about the Eucharist.

The icon as liturgical art is the visual means of veneration, conveying and giving support to the spiritual facts that underlie the whole liturgical drama of worship complementing the music and words already contained in the service. Appealing to our sense of sight, the icon testifies theologically to the principle of the incarnation. In the incarnation, God has displayed the supreme act of self-portrayal by becoming flesh in his Son. The incarnation is the icon or image of the invisible God and therefore reflects the glory of God. It would be theologically accurate to say that God himself was the first icon maker, visibly reproducing himself in the likeness of his Son, and thereby has set the precedent for the veneration of the icon to give glory to himself within the unceasing life of the liturgy.

The church filled with the presence of the icons is a house of doxology. The church is the very image, the very icon, of the universe unfolding the Christian view of time and history. For the Orthodox believer, this Christian pattern is threefold: the first and highest on the scale is the heavenly and uncreated world of divine being; the second corresponds to the world as it was created in the beginning "a world which was lost through the 'fall' of man, and was 'reformed' through the incarnation and the whole cycle of events which make up the life of Christ, or the New Testament. The third level is that of human and terrestrial existence—not of this existence in its fallen state but as it has been or is in the process of being reformed through the redemptive action of the Saviour."[8] As the house of doxology, the church's primary obligation is to give glory to God for this unfolding theology of history—this *Heilsge-schichte* to which the church as a living icon gives witness.

The iconic nature of the Orthodox Church is seen within her architectural structure. The divine world is shown forth in the dome with the representation of Christ as Pantocrator (Ruler of All); on the squinches, the pendentives, and the upper parts of the walls are scenes dedicated to the life of Christ, to that reforming of the lost paradise, and which therefore correspond to the Holy Land, to the heavenly Jerusalem; and on the lower or secondary vaults and on the lower walls are images of the saints and martyrs, holy men and women who already have a part in the redeemed world.[9] The final focus of the iconic structure of the church finds the believer turning his gaze to the front and viewing squarely the iconostasis, the screen of icons that separates the sanctuary from the nave. "The screen, the curtain, and later the iconostasis separate the sanctuary from the nave and mark the borderline between two worlds: the extratemporal and the temporal. As time went by, the development of the sanctuary screen and its modification into a solid iconostasis was always precisely in the direction of an even greater revelation of the significance of this demarcation."[10] The aim of the iconostasis is not to divide the priesthood from the people, but rather to serve as the expression of the mutual interpenetration of the temporal and the eternal, of the sanctuary and the nave. It is from this perspective that the significance of the iconostasis should be viewed in the Eastern Church.

On the iconostasis, the worshiper views the principal icons of the faith, beginning with the icon of Christ to the right of the royal door and to the left the icon of Mary (Mother of God). Next to Christ is the icon of John the Baptist (the Forerunner) and beside Mary the icon of a saint to whom the church is dedicated. Above these principal icons, which are usually life-size, there are three or four rows of smaller icons varying among the different national churches in Orthodoxy. The usual order of these rows is as follows: "First a row of apostles, then a row of saints and martyrs, then a row of prophets, and finally a row of patriarchs of the Old Testament. Above the middle door there is usually the *deesis*, a repre-

sentation of Christ on his throne as ruler of the universe, with
Mary and John standing to his right and left, in poses indicating that they are interceding for men."[11] This succession of
images presents the celestial church to the congregation, and
corresponds precisely to the theological content of the Eucharistic liturgy.

Among the list of Orthodox saints that appear on the iconostasis, the Virgin Mary holds a special place of veneration and
honor. Unlike Roman Catholics, the Orthodox do not hold to
the immaculate conception of Mary, but do share belief in her
bodily assumption, though this is never considered to be
dogma as it is for Roman Catholics. Dogmas for the Orthodox
center upon the Trinity and the incarnation, chief areas of the
church's announcement and proclamation to the world, whereas the veneration of Mary belongs to the church's inner tradition. Mary's sainthood rests solidly on the fact that she is the
Mother of God. "In Orthodox services Mary is often mentioned, and on each occasion she is usually given her full title:
'Our All-Holy, immaculate, most blessed and glorified Lady,
Mother of God and Ever-Virgin Mary.' Here are included the
three chief epithets applied to Our Lady by the Orthodox
Church: *Theotokos* (Mother of God), *Aeiparthenos* (Ever-
Virgin), and *Panagia* (All-Holy). The first of these titles was
assigned to her by the third Ecumenical Council (Ephesus,
431), the second by the fifth Ecumenical Council (Constantinople, 553). The title *Panagia*, although never a subject of dogmatic definition, is accepted and used by all
Orthodox."[12]

In short, the visual theology of the icon places the Orthodox
worshiper in an entirely different setting from his Protestant
or even Catholic counterpart. It is only as the Westerner is
able to appreciate in some depth what the icon wishes to
express that he will begin to understand what was at stake in
the iconoclastic controversy of the eighth century and its relevance for our day.

Iconoclasm Updated

The iconoclastic controversy should not be regarded as an eighth-century controversy recorded in dusty church chronicles. The controversy is even today of concern to Orthodox and non-Orthodox alike. The controversy in its modern form is seen in the recent "death of God" discussions. The "death of God" theologians are extreme iconoclasts heralding prophetic judgment upon churchmen whose icons have become idols. Historically, it has been seen that neither iconoclasts nor iconodules in their extreme forms further the peace and unity of the church. Since the very nature of Biblical faith affirms that man is created in the "image of God" and that the "Word became flesh," the precedent has been well established for icons; but the Biblical faith also affirms the qualitative distinction between the creation and the Creator, the "wholly other" reality of God that will always elude man's comprehension and attempts at representation. Herein lies our difficulty and our hope in this earthly pilgrimage. We are called upon to be both iconoclast and iconodule! It has been the Christian church's failure both in the East and in the West to maintain this creative tension that marks the iconoclastic controversy of the eighth century as a contemporary issue.

Today's churchman, like his forefathers, pursues an endless quest for models, images, and icons to capture the reality of his eternal destiny. Yet the danger always remains that whatever the means of his expression—language, wood, metal, or something else—the believer may be building a pseudo iconostasis of gold coloring devoid of the Spirit and of life. Protestants, with their emphasis upon the spoken word, must realize that words are also icons. Words describe the reality of God and his disclosure of himself through his Son, but these very words can become idols which we worship in lieu of God himself. Theologizing and sermonizing can alter language into pseudo images with no correspondence to divine realities. We cannot avoid the tasks of theologizing or sermonizing, but this always includes a responsible risk. Within this context we must evaluate the current conversations on demythologizing, the new hermeneutics, and the "death of God" discourses.[13]

With this note of caution, let us examine that complicated and complex controversy of the eighth century. Actually, acceptance of the icon within worship and community life did not take place overnight; it evolved over a period of time. Finally, during the reign of Emperor Leo III, the question arose whether this veneration and dignity given to icons was essentially a matter of idolatry. This question resulted in more than 120 years of controversy (726–843) during which the iconoclasts were defeated by the iconodules in the seventh Ecumenical Council (787), and brought to a permanent settlement by Empress Theodora in 843. The final victory in favor of the use of the icons or Holy Images is known as the "Triumph of Orthodoxy" and is commemorated in a special service celebrated on "Orthodox Sunday"—the first Sunday in Lent. "During this service the true faith—Orthodoxy—is proclaimed, its defenders are honoured, and anathemas pronounced on all who attack the Holy Icons or the Seven General Councils:

> To those who reject the Councils of the Holy Fathers, and their traditions which are agreeable to divine revelation, and which the Orthodox Catholic Church piously maintains, Anathema! Anathema! Anathema!"[14]

The iconoclasts, in their opposition to icons, failed to take full account of the incarnation. The supposition of the iconoclasts was that matter was unholy—hence icons painted for the most part on wood or metal were subjecting the divine to a material plane. The scandal of the incarnation was really too radical a concept for the iconoclasts to accept. They sought to deify the very humanity of Jesus, and to do so is to betray the incarnation, which was a fusion of the divine and the human in a mysterious way. Thus there is a close connection between the iconoclast controversy and the earlier disputes about Christ's person. It was not simply a controversy over religious art, but over the entire meaning and implication of the incarnation and its consequent significance for man. "God took a material body, thereby proving that matter can be redeemed: 'The Word made flesh has deified the flesh,' said John of Damascus. God has 'deified' matter, making it 'spirit-bearing'; and if flesh became a vehicle of the Spirit, then so—through a different way—can wood and paint. The Orthodox doctrine of icons is bound up with the Orthodox belief that the whole of God's creation, material as well as spiritual, is to be redeemed and glorified."[15] Thus in the text read on the Sunday of the Triumph of Orthodoxy (found in the Kontakion) are the following words:

The indefinable word of the Father made Himself definable, having taken flesh of Thee, O Mother of God, and having refashioned the soiled image to its former estate, has suffused it with Divine beauty. But confessing salvation we show it forth in deed and word.[16]

The very text of the Kontakion discloses the connection between the icon and Christological dogma, the basing of the icon on the divine incarnation. "In depicting the Saviour, we do not depict either His Divine or His human nature, but His Person in which both these natures are incomprehensibly combined. We depict His Person, since the icon can only be a personal, hypostatical image, while (in) nature, 'essence has no independent existence, but is seen in persons.' The icon is connected with the original, not on the strength of an identity between its own nature and his nature, but because it depicts his person and bears his name, which connects the icon with the person it represents and gives the possibility of communion with him and the possibility of knowing him. Owing to this connection, 'homage paid to the image is transmitted to the original,' say the holy Fathers and the Oecumenical Council, quoting the words of Basil the Great. Inasmuch as the icon is an image, it cannot be consubstantial with the original; otherwise it would cease to be an image and would become the original, would be one nature with it. The icon differs from the original precisely by the fact that it has another, different nature, for 'the representation is one thing, and that which it represents is another.' In other words, although the two subjects are essentially different, there exists between them a known connection, a certain participation of the one in the other."[17] Thus we can say that the icon is not so much a representation of the Deity as a spiritual vision captured by the artisan's participation (and also the worshiper's) in the divine life. The icon is a testimony and a concrete sign of sanctification known as *theosis* or "deification" to the Orthodox.

The worshiper contemplating the icon becomes the point of reference. He is conscious that the icon is addressing him in his Christian pilgrimage toward *theosis*. The skillfully distorted shapes of the icon express the metamorphosis and transfiguration at present taking place in the very life of the believer. The world itself is in the process of becoming a cosmos, an expression of beauty heralding the new creation in the Spirit. In the icons, the believer is able to synthesize external forms and the internal spiritual dimension in all its depth. "Instead of the 'prison of the soul' the body becomes the soul's temple. It is lightly drawn, or rather hinted at by the sober folds of the clothes whose dryness of line draws no attention to the anatomy but conveys the impression of a divinized and heavenly body. Even nakedness is shown in icons as the clothing of glory, not a display of the flesh but a revelation of the spirit. A saint is clothed in space and the nakedness of Adam."[18] The dynamics of deification or *theosis* are at the very heart of Orthodox spirituality, and the icons serve a key role as symbolic prototypes of those who have undergone transfiguration and address themselves to the worshiper in his earthly pilgrimage.

In summary, the emphasis has been upon the icon as an extension of the principle of incarnation, revealing and transmitting visually the realization of the patristic formula, "God became Man so that man should become God." Ultimately, the art and meaning of the icon aims "to transform the person who moves towards it so that he no longer distinguishes between the worlds of eternity and time, of spirit and matter, of the divine and the human, but sees both as one Reality, both as aspects of that unaged and ageless image-bearing light in which all things live, move, and have their being."[19] Our discussion must now consider the implications of this visual theology for the entire Christian *oikoumenē*. Does Orthodoxy's historic commitment to icons have something definite to say to Protestants and Catholics who with their Eastern brethren live in an age of visual technology? Is there not a need for a visual theology in today's cosmopolis?

Mission of a Visual Theology

For Protestants, there is no theological visual art that is not susceptible to idolatry. Protestants, unlike the Orthodox, have tended to be iconoclastic. To speak of a mission in connection with a visual theology is tantamount to promoting idolatry and undermining the proclamation of the word. Protestants do not find in the incarnation of Jesus Christ a license to permit icons. The incarnation is interpreted primarily as an event that cannot be either reproduced or repeated. It has a quality of once-for-allness about it. The distinguished Protestant theologian Karl Barth stated: "Since God in His deity is human, this culture must occupy itself neither with God in Himself nor with man in himself but with the man-encountering God and the God-encountering man and with their dialogue and history, in which their communion takes place and comes to its fulfillment. For this reason theology can think and speak only as it looks at Jesus Christ and from the vantage point of what He is. It cannot introduce Him. Neither can it bring about that dialogue, history, and communion. It does not have the disposition of these things. It is dependent upon the Holy Scripture, according to which the covenant is *in full effect* and in which Jesus Christ *witnesses to Himself.* It hears this witness. It trusts it and is satisfied with it."[20] It should then not surprise the Orthodox that many Protestants find it difficult to appreciate icons. An icon, for the Orthodox, participates in the event and is almost a re-creation of that event existentially for the believer, while religious pictures or paintings for Protestants within the context of the church are really nothing more than illustrations of object lessons.

In the West, the theologian has instructed and even limited the artist, whereas in the "East an iconographer is a charismatic who contemplates the liturgical mysteries and instructs the theologian."[21] Protestantism in its encounter with Orthodoxy has the opportunity, although aware of the dangers of idolatry, of supporting verbal reflection of the gospel with visual reflection of the gospel. This will enhance the church's witness to the whole man. "Iconography has the character of 'visual reflection of theology'; its contemplation translates the intense charity, the 'ontological tenderness' of the great spiritual masters towards every creature. 'The divine Teacher,' says Maximus, 'feeds men eucharistically with knowledge of the ultimate destinies of the world.' An immense parable, the world offers a reading of 'God's poetry' written in its flesh. The icon deciphers it in the light of the liturgy, and it is from this source that the joyful cosmicism of Orthodoxy comes."[22] A visual theology, in short, has the possibility of enhancing the communication within the sanctuary; it can be a source of idolatry as well. Tomorrow's ecumenical theologizing must confront this creative tension.

The technique of iconography itself evokes the visual make-up and impact upon the believer. The basic materials which enter into the making of an icon in their totality represent the fullest participation of the visible world. That is to say, the material elements stem from the vegetable, mineral, and animal worlds. "The most fundamental of these materials (water, chalk, pigments, egg . . .) are taken in their natural form, merely purified and prepared, and by the work of his hands man brings them to serve God. In this sense the words of the Prophet David, spoken by him at the blessing of the materials for the building of the temple, 'All things are thine, and of thine own have we given thee' (I Chron. 29:14) are still more applicable to the icon where matter serves to express the image of God. But these words acquire their highest significance in the Liturgy at the offering of the Holy Gifts to be transformed into the very Body and Blood of Christ: 'Thine own of Thine own we offer to Thee, in all and for all.' "[23] Matter offered in the icon as a gift to God by man, in its way further underlines the liturgic meaning of the icon. The materials employed in the icons are but another expression of belief in the materialism of Christianity—in God the Creator who is also God the Redeemer.

Our discussion on the art and mission of the icon must include another mission for the icon which the East can far more advantageously fulfill than can the West. The suggestion is actually a reversal of strategy practiced for centuries by Eastern Christians who live in Islamic areas.[24] Kenneth Cragg, the recognized Islamic expert and missionary, puts forth the suggestion that the Orthodox use of icons may spell a possible bridge of communication to the Islamic culture which abhors all forms of idolatry, but which within its very framework has the visual need of art. Cragg, conscious of the presence of Orthodoxy in Islamic areas of predominance, raises the vital question: "Can we not break through Islam's supposed, but unreal, independence of the artistic to a deeper and more humble understanding of the glad Christian involvement in it? For if we can, we may be nearer than we have ever been to penetrating Muslim thought with the meaning of the Incarnation."[25] If we take seriously and earnestly the Christian claim of the incarnation as the Orthodox do, then we can never doubt or reject the claim that there is spiritual disunity between the visible and the invisible, the divine and the human. The Islamic warning of lurking idolatry in association with the incar-

nation stems from the Muslim fear of man's chronic temptation
to take the image for the substance. This fear is well founded,
e.g., the golden calf in the days of Moses and Aaron. On the
other hand, the Orthodox perhaps may be able to point out to
their Muslim neighbors that to deny the incarnation, in the
name of this fear, is really to deny creation the role of the
visible, to miss the entire sacramental meaning of the world
and to invite a nemesis of unreality.[26]

Islam, like Protestantism, is iconoclastic, but nevertheless it
does not escape the necessity of sacramentalizing. "Its postures
at prayer, its Qiblah towards Mecca, its garb on pilgrimage,
its very calligraphy, even the very absence of the pictorial—
all proceed by enlisting the senses in the expression of Divine-
human things. Since the sacramental is necessarily there if
there is to be religion—it had better, and safer, be there
consciously and theologically. Can Islamic thought not hold
firmly to its fears of the perversities of art, without refusing
and excluding its validities? Might it not learn to look not
merely with a new tolerance, but with a new eagerness, upon
the symbols of Christian faith which, as concepts, it has so long
controversially despised? . . . For this very reason there is a
deep likeness between what happens in a great work of art and
what the Christian faith believes God is doing in Christ. . . .
For great works of art, in any form, have always a double
nature. There is the concrete event and the transcendent meaning: there is the material ground (be it paint or stone or other
'base') yielded into the artistic genius and there is the soul of
the artist there self-expressed and self-fulfilled. What he is, is
inseparable from what he does: what he means is manifest in
what he shapes. The tangible and visible are the home and
residence of the spiritual and the eternal. Can we not see the
Incarnation in these terms as the self-revelation of God indwelling the fashion of the living and crucified Christ, Who is
'the express image of God's person, the outshining of His
glory' (Heb. 1:3), 'the image of the invisible God' (Col.

1:15)? Is not this in truth what the Gospel means when it proclaims that 'the Word became flesh'?"[27]

Thus Cragg believes from his study of Islam that "Islamic
attitudes to art in worship may be seen as all of one piece with
its misunderstanding of the Incarnation. . . . The Muslim fear
of idolatry is always sound. But the security against it is not—
in banning the artists (any more than God's unity is safeguarded by vetoing the Incarnation): it is in a true recognition
of Him in undivided love. That love may include unashamedly
the help and benediction of the senses and the arts. It is when
men cease to offer adoration that they begin to practice idolatry. Their adoration of God will be not the less but the more
true, for their delight in His creation. For the Christian that
delight is all focused and completed in wonder at the marvel
that our earthly context has seen and known and handled His
incarnate Presence."[28] It is clear that the liturgical art of the
icon in Orthodoxy can potentially go far in giving the Orthodox a theological basis to relate to their Islamic neighbors
from a position of strength, for they have suffered too long in
silence as a minority people. Out of Orthodoxy's traditional
strength in the art and use of the icon lies the possibility of
enhancing the Christian church's dialogue with the Islamic
world.

Chapter X

The Holy Spirit
in East and West

The underlying confessional quarrels between Eastern and Western Christendom are to a large extent caused by the absence of a common pneumatological theology. The purpose here is to provide a brief introduction for Western Christians to the role of the Holy Spirit in Eastern Orthodox theology, in the hope that someday a common pneumatological theology will be achieved. Furthermore, we in the West have a great opportunity to enrich ourselves by bringing Orthodoxy to the forefront of our discussions of the "Doctrine of the Spirit," since this Eastern branch of Christendom has long been regarded as the *eschatologically oriented church of the Spirit.* Orthodoxy has long considered herself to be the holy church indwelt by the Spirit. The late Vladimir Lossky, a respected contemporary Orthodox theologian, rightly characterizes the theology and worship of the Eastern Church "as a witness to the fullness of the Holy Spirit—to this Person who, though He fills all things and brings all things to their ultimate fulfillment, yet remains Himself unknown."[1] It is with much significance, then, that we examine the Orthodox understanding of the Spirit: first, historically (in reference to the Filioque); second, sacramentally (in explanation of the Epiclesis); and third, personally (regarding the meaning and implication of *theosis*).

The Holy Spirit and the Trinity

The Filioque controversy has served historically as the chief event for the parting of the ways between East and West.[2] There are important political and social ramifications behind the controversy,[3] but for our purposes the theological aspect of the issue is of immediate concern. Does the Holy Spirit proceed from the Father and the Son (Filioque) or from the Father alone? The Eastern Church rejects the later addition of the Filioque to the Nicene Creed. For the Orthodox, this addition, which might seem technical and obscure, has grave implications. "From the viewpoint of traditional Orthodox theology there can be but one rejoinder to this: technical and obscure it undoubtedly is, like most questions of Trinitarian theology; but it is not trivial. Since belief in the Trinity lies at the very heart of the Christian faith, a tiny difference in Trinitarian theology is bound to have repercussions upon every aspect of Christian life and thought."[4] What, then, is the root of Orthodoxy's rejection of the Filioque?

Patriarch Photius saw two possible heresies in the addition of Filioque to the Creed: the doctrine of double procession of the Holy Spirit (i.e., the Filioque) points "either to a 'Manichaean' division of the godhead into two sources, out of whom the third agent proceeds; or a Neo-Platonic scale of being, in which the Holy Spirit is one degree further removed from the Father than the Son."[5] Photius sought to follow the teachings of the Cappadocian fathers, stressing that since God is one, the Father is also one. From the viewpoint of Orthodoxy, the Filioque destroys this *essence of oneness* in the Godhead. "The Godhead is, to speak concisely, undivided in separate Persons";[6] for the persons of the Trinity are both a "community and unity."[7] The early fathers were speaking in behalf of the *homoousion* tradition with its formula "one *ousia* in three *hypostaseis*," with special stress upon the "wholehearted recognition of the *homoousion* of the Spirit,"[8] and thereby avoiding all traces of subordination as later indicated by the addition

of the Filioque. Orthodoxy favors and seeks to maintain the
tension of unity in diversity and diversity in unity as expressed
in the mystery of the Holy Trinity. There are personal distin-
guishing characteristics of each person in the Trinity, but
there is also a cohesive unity in the Godhead. From the Orthodox standpoint, "the Father is the 'cause' or 'source' of Godhead, He is the principle (*archē*) of unity among the three;
and it is in this sense that Orthodoxy talks of the 'monarchy'
of the Father. The other two persons trace their origin to the
Father and are defined in terms of their relation to Him. The
Father is the source of Godhead, born of none and proceeding
from none; the Son is born of the Father from all eternity
('before all ages,' as the Creed says); the Spirit proceeds from
the Father from all eternity."[9] It can be readily observed that
the principle of unity in Orthodoxy is linked to the Father and
is therefore a personal rather than an abstract principle of
unity, as is found in Western thinking.[10]

The traditional formula "one *ousia* in three *hypostaseis*" was
so constructed to uphold the mysterious tension between
ousia and *hypostaseis*. The "Greek East" chose to approach the
dogma of the Trinity by means of the three persons (*hypostaseis*) and then to pass on to the one nature, whereas the
"Latin West" chose the opposite course—from the one substance (*ousia*) to the three persons. Actually, either course is
permissible and "orthodox," providing that undue emphasis is
not placed upon one at the expense of the other. In fact, this
was the aim of the traditional formula. If the balance between
persons and nature—between being absolutely unique and yet
absolutely identical—is upset, the result will be either a tendency toward tritheism with emphasis upon *persons*, or a
tendency toward a Sabellian unitarianism with an emphasis
upon an abstract substance, resulting in a Scholastic and philosophical approach to God.[11]

The Greeks noted this latter tendency in the Latins, while
asserting that they themselves had overcome the opposite
tendency toward tritheism by maintaining "that the principle

of unity in the Trinity is the person of the Father. As Principle of the other two persons, the Father is at the same time the Source of the relations whence the hypostases receive their distinctive characteristics. In causing the persons to proceed, he lays down their relations of origin—generalization and procession—in regard to the unique principle of Godhead. This is why the East has always opposed the Western interpolation of *filioque* which seems to impair the monarchy of the Father: either one is forced to destroy the unity by acknowledging two principles of Godhead, or one must ground the unity primarily on the common nature, which thus overshadows the persons and transforms them into relations within the unity of the essence."[12] It is in this context that the Greek fathers emphasized that there is one God, since there is one Father. Thus it can be seen more clearly why Orthodoxy insists upon the eternal procession of the Holy Spirit from the Father alone and not from the combination of the Father and the Son (Filioque). This latter would endanger the monarchy of the Father as well as subordinate the role of the Holy Spirit and the uniqueness of the Trinity. That is to say, "filioquism confuses the persons, and destroys the proper balance between unity and diversity in the Godhead. The oneness of the deity is emphasized at the expense of His threeness; God is regarded too much in terms of abstract essence and too little in terms of concrete personality."[13]

Not only is this excess of emphasis upon the unity of God objected to by Orthodoxy, but also the resulting subordination of the Holy Spirit. Therefore, Eastern Orthodoxy has long thought that Western theology in theory and in practice has given insufficient attention to the work of the Holy Spirit in relation to the Trinity, to the church, and to the daily tasks of the Christian in the world.[14] The Orthodox look to a passage such as John 15:26, "But when the Counselor comes, whom I shall send to you from the Father, even the Spirit of truth, who proceeds from the Father, he will bear witness to me," and thereby believe themselves justified on Scriptural grounds in saying that the Holy Spirit proceeds from the Father alone, and that Scripture nowhere seems to suggest that the Holy Spirit proceeds from the Father *and the Son*.[15]

The word "proceed" has been used several times. What do the Orthodox mean by "proceed" in reference to the Holy Spirit? Unless this term "is properly understood," says Timothy Ware, "nothing is understood. The Church believes that Christ underwent two births, the one eternal, the other at a particular point in time: he was born of the Father 'before all ages,' and born of the Virgin Mary in the days of Herod, King of Judaea, and of Augustus, Emperor of Rome. In the same way a firm distinction must be drawn between the *eternal procession* of the Holy Spirit, and the *temporal mission*, the sending of the Spirit to the world: the one concerns the relation existing from all eternity within the Godhead, the other concerns the relation of God to creation. Thus when the West says that the Spirit proceeds from the Father and the Son, and when Orthodoxy says that He proceeds from the Father alone, both sides are referring not to the outward action of the Trinity towards creation, but to certain eternal relations within the Godhead— relations which existed before ever the world was. But Orthodoxy, while disagreeing with the West is saying that, so far as the mission of the Spirit to the world is concerned, He is sent by the Son, and is indeed the 'Spirit of the Son.' "[16] Thus the implication is made that Western Christendom has in fact confused the eternal and temporal dimension of procession regarding the Spirit, thus disrupting the balance of the Trinity and misinterpreting the Biblical witness. The historic emphasis of Orthodoxy upon the apophatic and mysterious procession of the Holy Spirit from all eternity in opposition to the Filioque has contributed to Orthodoxy's distinctive place in Christendom as the "Church of the Holy Spirit."

When the different emphasis of the two Trinitarian doctrines (between East and West) has been clearly seen, "it will be understood why the East has always defended the ineffable, apophatic character of the procession of the Holy Spirit from the Father, unique source of the persons, against a more rational doctrine which, in making of the Father and the Son a common principle of the Holy Spirit, places the common nature above the persons; a doctrine which tends to weaken the hypostases by confounding the persons of Father and Son in the natural act of spiration, and in making of the Holy Spirit a connection between the two."[17] From a Western view, Prof. George S. Hendry, of Princeton, admits that the interpolation of the Filioque "was a false solution to a real problem. It satisfied the immediate concern of the Christian mind to identify the Spirit that is known in the experience of salvation as the Spirit of Christ, but it raises grave difficulties when it is extended to the operations of the Trinity in creation."[18]

Interestingly, the Roman Church allows the Uniate Churches of the East in communion with Rome to omit the Filioque in their affirmation of the Creed. Furthermore, the unofficial conference at Bonn in 1875 by some important segments of Anglicanism, Old Catholics, and Orthodox agreed to be willing to repudiate the Filioque in the interest of furthering unity and communion with Eastern Orthodoxy. Orthodoxy has a greater sympathetic audience for its position on the Filioque than would be at first suspected by churchmen in both the East and the West. This controversy which has raged for so many years must be viewed as something more than a hairsplitting exercise among theologians; it concerns the very basis of our Trinitarian faith.

The Holy Spirit and the Church

Long ago but sounding refreshingly contemporary, Irenaeus wrote: "Where the Church is, there is the Spirit of God; and where the Spirit of God is, there is the Church."[19]

Orthodoxy has held tenaciously to this theological maxim, for she has regarded the church, the body of Christ, as the temple and dwelling place of the Spirit. Thus the Holy Spirit might be described in this Orthodox context as the Spirit of

the church, for it is the Holy Spirit who rules and dwells in
the church and among the fellow Christians, the communion
of saints who make up the church. Orthodoxy associates the
Church and Spirit organically together and views the individual Christian as one who receives the gift of the Spirit
within the context of the church and not apart from the
church. An individualistic pietism or Pentecostal experience,
be it glossolalia, healing, or some other charismatic manifestation, has validity only within the context of the church wherein
dwells the Holy Spirit, whose Lordship rules the church.

This is not to say that the Orthodox are adverse to diversity
within the body of Christ. From the Orthodox standpoint, "the
Holy Spirit is a Spirit of freedom. While Christ unites us, the
Holy Spirit ensures our infinite diversity in the Church: at
Pentecost the tongues of fire were 'cloven' or divided, descend-
ing *separately* upon each one of those present. The gift of the
Spirit is a gift to the Church, but it is at the same time a
personal gift, appropriated by each in his own way. 'There are
diversities of gifts, but the same Spirit' (I Cor. 12:4). Life in
the Church does not mean the ironing out of human variety,
nor the imposition of a rigid and uniform pattern upon all
alike, but the exact opposite. The saints, so far from displaying
a drab monotony, have developed the most vivid and distinctive personalities. It is not holiness but evil which is dull."[20]
Orthodoxy is actually open to a wide diversity of the Spirit's
leading.

The centrality of the Spirit's witness is expressed simply but
eloquently in Orthodoxy. Within the church's worship there
are only a few prayers directly addressed to the Holy Spirit.
"The chief expression of the Church's piety towards the Spirit
is found in the *Pentēkostarion* (the collection of services for
the season of Pentecost). But there are two prayers, used at all
seasons which require our attention. . . . One opens most of
the Orthodox services and corresponds after a fashion to the
Latin *Veni Creator:*

Heavenly King, Comforter, Spirit of truth, who are everywhere and fillest all, treasure of graces and giver of life, O come and dwell in us; cleanse us from all defilement and save our souls, O gracious One.

"The other prayer is:

O Lord, who at the third hour, didst send down Thy most Holy Spirit upon Thine Apostles, do not take Him away from us, O Gracious One, but renew us who pray unto Thee."[21]

In addition to the above prayers, there is the "Epiclesis of the Holy Spirit" ("The Invocation of the Holy Spirit"), given at the time of the Eucharist. The Epiclesis itself points to the descent of the Holy Spirit to change the elements into the body and blood of the Lord. The priest or bishop repeats the Epiclesis, or invocation, quietly, but sometimes within the full hearing of the congregation, with the following words:

> Send down Thy Holy Spirit upon us and upon
> these gifts here set forth:
> And make this bread the Precious Body of Thy
> Christ,
> And that which is in the cup, the Precious
> Blood of Thy Christ,
> Changing them by Thy Holy Spirit. Amen,
> Amen, Amen.[22]

Following this prayer, the priest and deacon immediately prostrate themselves before the Holy Gifts, which have now been consecrated for holy use. "It will be evident that the 'moment of consecration' is understood somewhat differently by the Orthodox and the Roman Catholic Churches. According to Latin theology, the consecration is effected by the Words of Institution: 'This is my Body . . .' 'This is my Blood . . .' According to Orthodox theology, the act of consecration is not complete until the end of the *Epiclesis*, and worship of the Holy Gifts before this point is condemned by the Orthodox Church as 'artolatry' (bread worship)."[23]

"The Epiclesis of the Holy Spirit," for the Orthodox, expresses an unbroken communion with his Lord in the spiritual worship of the church, the body of Christ. For the Orthodox, it is not the sacrifice of the cross that is offered again, but the "remembrance" of the one body, the one ecclesia, the one Christ, whose sacrificial body is mysteriously recalled again by the Spirit of the church who invites the believer to a deeper mystical participation in the life of the Holy Spirit. The priest who symbolically represents the congregation and his Christ at the "moment of consecration" dramatically and yet passively presents the once-for-all *leitourgos* offering of Christ himself as the dearest sacrifice of God for man. The ultimate aim of Orthodox worship is the glorification of God through the spiritual renewal and remaking of man through the Holy Spirit, in the Eucharistic and eschatologically oriented environs of the church, which is the home of the Spirit.[24]

The Holy Spirit and the Christian

Orthodox spirituality for the individual believer is rooted and grounded in Orthodox ecclesiology. The Spirit and the church are organically linked together and only within this binding relationship can the Christian grow and mature in his spiritual development. The process of becoming holy or sanctified takes place within the very heart and life of the Eucharistic worship of the church. This growth in spirituality in Orthodox theology is known as *theosis* and begins with the new-born child who is brought into the household of faith to receive Baptism, Confirmation, and the Eucharist. "The Orthodox Church feels that the process of Christian initiation, involving Baptism, Confirmation, and Communion in the Holy Mysteries, constitutes an inseparable whole, which ought to be conferred on each new Christian as such, whether child or adult."[25]

Once the child has been received within the fellowship of the church and has received the sacraments, the process of reestablishing and renewing and becoming the new man "in Christ" has begun. This process is known as *theosis*. It has at times been described as the unfolding "divinization" or "deification" of man and has thereby been unjustly criticized by Western theologians. On the contrary, *theosis* does not in any way point to a mystical union of divine and human nature which might result in the absorption of the latter by the former. Rather, *theosis* seeks to express the growing and dynamic unfolding, since the child's reception within the fellowship of the church, of a deepening awareness of the grace of the Triune God through the work and person of the Holy Spirit in the child's life, as the child lives within the communion of the church. The Holy Spirit enables us to pass from the objective redemption given and experienced in the sacraments at infancy, to the subjective appropriation by man, leading ultimately to a complete transformation and newness of life for man. The restoration of human nature to its first and former state—the sinlessness of unfallen Adam—is the goal of *theosis* or sanctification[26] under the inspiration and guidance of the Holy Spirit. "Therefore, we can say further that the Paraclete is not only a subjective agent to realize in man the objective salvation alone; He is also the power of Revelation and its fulfillment. Fulfillment means rendering the possibility of being in Christ a reality in Christ. . . . If Christ's revelation reconciles us, in the fulfillment of the Holy Spirit, we are invited to walk in the newness of the Spirit (Rom. 6:4; 7:5)."[27] In short, the outcome of *theosis* is to reinstate man's true humanity seen and known by the apostles in the incarnation of Jesus Christ.[28] *Theosis* points to the re-creation of the Christian into the image of the incarnate One.

The role of the Holy Spirit in Orthodoxy is too vast a topic to have said all within the span of this chapter. However, the material submitted sufficiently indicates: (1) that the West owes a great deal to Orthodoxy's historic stand against the Filioque; (2) that the role of the Holy Spirit in the Eucharist and worship of the church leads the Orthodox believer to the edge of mystery and beyond rational explanation so desirable to the Western mind; and (3) that the Spirit of the church personally engages and orients its members toward a new *household of humanity,* which indeed is the aim of Christians everywhere. Increased awareness of the need for a common pneumatological theology for East and West will further efforts toward our common goal—a new humanity in Christ.

Chapter XI

Spirituality, Monasticism, and Relevance

In the summer of 1962, a unique conference on Eastern and Western spirituality took place at the Ecumenical Institute near Geneva, Switzerland.[1] The participants of the conference were Orthodox, Protestants, and Roman Catholics. Their presence underscored the genuine concern all Christians have for an authentic spirituality that transcends the parochial limitations of our several traditions.

Spirituality: Eastern and Western

The word "spirituality," like the word "trinity," does not appear per se in Scripture. Words similar to the idea of spirituality are found in I Cor. 12:1; 14:1; and Eph. 6:12. Actually, the category of spirituality is neutral; its nature is noted only when we add a modifier. "Christian" spirituality indicates a positive connotation of the term. Christian spirituality in practice is a personal affair rather than a codified ethic. Its sources have been Biblical and ecclesiastical. It has received explicit sacramental sanction through the events of Baptism and the Eucharist. These two sacraments are the ecumenical signs of God's presence for all Christians, witnessing visibly to the apostolic character of the Christian fellowship. In the life of the church and through active participation in the sacraments, the individual believer receives nourishment and growth in the meaning and depth of Christian spirituality.

The sacraments of spirituality—Baptism and the Eucharist —remind the believer of the purpose of the church. " 'The Church exists not alone for mission but also for worship, for delight in God's goodness and mercy, for awe in his glorious presence'; again, on the basis of Ex. 19:5–6 and I Peter 2:9–10, 'this is given by God as his act inaugurating a new relationship with his people for other peoples "that you may declare the wonderful deeds (praises) of him who called you out of darkness into his marvelous light" ' (I Peter 2:9–10)."[2] Christians, in both the East and the West, can subscribe to such a Biblical and sacramental basis for Christian spirituality. Our ecclesiological interpretations of the Biblical and the sacramental divide us and cause us to question the authenticity of each other's spirituality.

The aim of Christian spirituality, in the East as well as in the West, is growth in the sanctified life—a life of praise and thanksgiving. This ecumenically shared goal can be one of the major arteries toward Christian unity. "Unity is realized when church people study their spiritual life in Christ, regarding this study and discussion as a calling of the Spirit towards a new engagement in the Church everywhere, transcending geographical, ethnic and political boundaries."[3] The concern for Christian spirituality is not only urgent in the secularized climate of today, but it is an ecumenical task that holds great promise for further confrontations among divergent traditions.

What are some of these divergent or contrasting strains of thought and tendencies in Eastern and Western spirituality? Beginning with a shared common origin in Christ, the patristic tradition of the East and the Augustinian tradition of the West formed their interior lives along different theological motifs. Eastern spirituality is characterized by ontological oneness with the Creator, and looks suspiciously Gnostic and Neoplatonic to the West. The West tends to be psychological and anthropological, aware of the eternal gulf and discontinuity between the Creator and his creature, which characterizes its spiritual tradition. The Eastern concept of *theosis* seeks to bridge this gulf between man and God. The dynamics of *theosis* seeks to deify or restore to union man's relationship to God as it was intended in the beginning. Man created in the *imago Dei* participates in divine realities. The only limit to man's nature is determined by the nature of God, which is essentially unknowable to the human mind. *Theosis* does not imply that man will displace God, but rather that man's nature is to grow into the fullness of God's glory. The dynamics of *theosis* are very much akin to the dynamics of sanctification in Western theologizing. The aim of each is to give a more lasting service of doxology to the Father and Creator of us all.

Thus contemporary Orthodox theologians, following their patristic tradition, in speaking of *theosis* use phrases similar to that of Athanasius, "God became man so that man might become God." This is not blasphemy but a search for an understanding of Christian spirituality at the highest theological plane. This is difficult for Protestants to grasp, with their underlying iconoclastic desire to uproot any hint of idolatry. The Orthodox outlook on *theosis* is no easy exaltation of man at the expense of God; rather, the Orthodox bring a cosmic dimension to Christian spirituality in line with the majesty and greatness of God himself. *Theosis* offers the believer the possibility and the promise that he "may return to his original relationship of communion with his God in order to recapture his true humanity and establish a right relationship with his fellowman in all realms of social life. *Theosis* in patristic thought is in no way a static, ontological idea or affirmation of the divinization of man, but it points to the final goal, to the possibility opened by faith for a man in this world as a new creation, transcending the normal conduct imposed by fallen nature and its laws. In this optimistic anthropology, the notion of *theosis* draws the attention of the saved man to his final purpose, which coincides with the central event of the gospel, the risen Lord in his church, and not with any abstract concept of resurrection."[4]

Theosis brings a cosmic dimension to redemption, for man sees himself as *homotheos*, whose purpose and destiny in the cosmos is to become by the grace of God, a son of God.

The individual believer's model and goal of spirituality is revealed in Christ, the Son of God. Human nature is consubstantial with the human nature of Christ. The East views humanity as permeated by the Divine, whereas the West sees humanity as ascending toward the Divine. Through Christ, for the Easterner, the whole of mankind participates in the Divine. Divinization, or deification, is a process and is achieved when the whole person achieves a harmony of body and spirit with God. The goal is to have the mind absorbed into the heart. The famous Jesus prayer identified with Hesychasm[5] is employed as an aid; the simple prayer states: "O Lord Jesus Christ, Son of God, have mercy upon me a sinner." This prayer is repeated many times with greater and greater concentration. By means of the prayer, Christ himself enters the heart of the believer and enlightens the individual's whole being on his pilgrimage toward a sanctified life.

The sanctified life in Orthodoxy is preoccupied in its contemplation with the incarnation and resurrection and the implications of these events for the spiritual life of the believer. Meditation of this kind has been characterized in the East as *theologia gloriae*, while Western spirituality and theologizing has been depicted as centered in *theologia crucis*. The later heritage of both Roman Catholics and Protestants has emphasized the imitation of his passion and the implications of his death for our salvation. Thomas à Kempis' *Imitation of Christ* is one of the best-known examples of Latin spirituality. Eastern spirituality and mysticism "is not interested in the life on this earth of Jesus Christ or in the idea of imitating his passions. The idea of stigmata is likewise foreign to it. It is far less anthropogenic than Western Christian mysticism; it is far less concerned with man's complex life on earth, with his struggle in life. The object of contemplation is not humanity, but the

divinity of Jesus Christ. As a result, the East has almost none of these confessions, diaries, autobiographies, accounts of the spiritual life of saints and mystics which are so common in the West. St. Augustine's idea that a knowledge of God is attainable through a knowledge of the human soul is equally foreign to the East. Thus Eastern mysticism is less dialogical and less dramatic than Western mysticism."[6] There is, instead, a maximizing of the eschatological and pneumatic in the East to a height not known in the West.

There is also a greater tendency for intellectual concentration and abstraction in the West than in the East. However, in the fourteenth century, Byzantine mystics such as St. Simeon, the New Theologian, exhibited a closeness to Western types such as St. John of the Cross. In Simeon "there is a dialogue between the human soul and Christ. But for all his peculiarities he remains representative of Eastern mysticism, blending in himself the intellectualist mysticism of gnosis with the affective mysticism of *Eros*."[7] Even in Simeon, however, Western phenomena such as stigmata are missing in Eastern thought. "Nor do disease and physical suffering play such an important part as they do in Catholic mysticism. The Orthodox East, and especially Russia, loves St. Francis as the saint who most nearly fulfilled the Gospel image of Christ. But there were traits of Western chivalry in St. Francis which are not to be found in St. Seraphim of Sarov, a typical representative of Eastern mysticism with its ideal of illumination and the divinization of the creature."[8] In short, Eastern spirituality is primarily centered in the resurrection, and Western spirituality looks for its inspiration in the crucifixion.

There is, of course, Biblical truth in both *theologia gloriae* and *theologia crucis*. In both Eastern and Western theologizing the emphasis upon the one aspect by its very nature includes the other as well. The stress upon the resurrection and the victory of life in Christ integrally relates to his suffering and death on the cross. The tension between these two realities must be

maintained in any valid theology of spirituality. According to
Father Georges Florovsky: "The Cross itself is the sign of
glory. The Cross itself is regarded not so much as a climax of
Christ's humiliation, but rather as a disclosure of Divine might
and glory. . . . On the one hand, the whole *oikonomia* of Redemption is summed up in one comprehensive vision; the victory of Life. On the other, this *oikonomia* is related to the basic
predicament of the fallen man, to his existential situation, cul-
minating in his actualized 'mortality,' and the 'last enemy' is
identified, accordingly, as 'death.' It was this 'last enemy' that
had been defeated and abrogated on the tree of the Cross, *in
ara crucis.* The Lord of Life did enter the dark abyss of death,
and 'death' was destroyed by the flashes of His glory. This is
the main motive of the divine office on Easter Day in the Orthodox Church: 'trampling down death by death.' The phrase
itself is significant: Christ's death is itself a victory, Christ's
death dismisses man's mortality."[9] It is in this organic relationship between *theologia gloriae* and *theologia crucis* that a truly
ecumenical theology of spirituality should find its locus of
power and strength.

Monasticism and the Kingdom of the Spirit

With these broad generalizations of Eastern and Western
spirituality in mind, let us now focus more specifically upon
monasticism. Eastern monasticism has been the fountain that
has nourished Orthodox spirituality and has served as an early
prototype for the West. Monks have been the heroes and saints
of the Christian faith. Their presence has been a vivid reminder to all Christians of the eschatological reality of the
Christian faith, that we are all pilgrims whose goal is the Kingdom of the Spirit. Christians within and without the monastic
community have at times lost sight of that eschatological reality, and the vitality of the Christian witness has proportion-
ately declined and suffered as a result. Today, Mt. Athos, the

venerable shrine of Eastern monasticism first settled in the middle of the tenth century by the learned monk St. Athanasius, is threatened by extinction. Even though fewer in Orthodoxy are pursuing the monastic vocation and many of the remaining monks on Mt. Athos are quite old, the history of the past centuries shows that the Holy Mount has gone through similar periods of difficulty before and has experienced an astonishing capacity for survival.

The question that a Protestant can justifiably raise is whether or not monasticism is an anachronism today. Looking to the twenty-first century, Eastern and Western Christians are living together on a global island. On this island, the productivity of all inhabitants, including those who choose a monastic life, is being questioned. The Protestant monastic community at Taizé, France, has done much to improve the stereotyped image which most Protestants have of monasticism.[10] Indeed, the Taizé brothers have been a living bridge of ecumenicity with both the Orthodox and Roman Catholics, and their achievements have not gone unnoticed. Nevertheless, many still question the contribution toward Christian growth in grace through austere asceticism in monastic life.

An answer to the above inquiry might be the significant experience, in retrospect, of one monk on Mt. Athos:

How moved I am as I recall the service of Matins which I attended as a monk! A vessel of clay, beset with weakness, I was strongly attached to my night's sleep. But I said to myself, "Sleep is sweet, yet there is nothing sweeter than prayer"— and I got up. In winter time—and winter can be very severe on the Holy Mountain—I had to fight not only against my drowsy eyelids but against the bitter cold. And then I repeated the phrase of the Forty Martyrs, "The cold is bitter, but Paradise is sweet." So I hurried to church. The services are long and it is hard work to stand upright all the time. Often I began to give way at the knees; I dropped asleep standing up; sometimes I fell out of my stall. But I never abandoned the service, and for my efforts I was richly rewarded from Heaven. I sailed upon an ocean of spiritual joy, and felt that I stood already in the antechamber of celestial blessedness.[11]

The monk whose testimony is quoted is now serving as a bishop. Orthodoxy has had a rich heritage of outstanding bishops who first practiced ascetics in the monasteries. Monastic asceticism has been the training school for ecclesiastical leadership in Orthodoxy. For the Orthodox monk, the practice of asceticism teaches obedience and faithfulness to God. Dionysios, Metropolitan of Trikka and Staghi, testifies again:

Obedience is like oxygen to a monk. Without oxygen a man cannot breathe, but is asphyxiated and dies; and in the same way without obedience a monk dies, from the point of view of the true monastic life. Obedience is life, and disobedience death. I recall how my spiritual father, to test my obedience, told me to go and dig in the garden, although I was altogether unfamiliar with any type of agricultural work, while on other occasions he told me to go and carry wood. Many times I seethed inwardly and was tempted to rebel, but I controlled myself, reflecting that obedience leads to humility and purity of heart, and remembering the pattern set by our Lord, who was "obedient to death, even death on a cross." (Phil. 2:8.)[12]

Monastic asceticism is literally an exercise, a spiritual gymnastics training for Christlike obedience. The word "ascetic" appears only once in the New Testament, in Acts 24:16, when the apostle Paul appeals to the Roman Governor, Felix, in the following terms: "So I always take pains [from *askeō:* "to practice patience to the limit"] to have a clear conscience toward God and toward men." There are many other inferences from the Gospels and the epistles warning the disciples and followers of Jesus to stand firm in their faith and to press on in their pilgrimage for the eschatological goal in Jesus Christ. Monastic asceticism underscores the spiritual warfare located in the very depths of man's heart. "St. Theophanus the Recluse wrote: "This spiritual combat should never be interrupted. It must be constantly resumed. If you fall, do not despair. Get up again with the

firm resolve not to fall again. And continue the struggle.' "¹³
Monastic withdrawal should not be interpreted by the observer as contempt for the world but, rather, as the necessary
retreat into the desert, to an island or some other place of
solitude, to better prepare oneself as a disciplined follower of
Christ. A seeking for solitude was considered the necessary
starting point for entering the Kingdom of the Spirit with joy.

Monastic asceticism itself has actually been practiced in
several forms. On Mt. Athos four major types of monks have
coexisted, each with its distinct form of asceticism. The earliest of the four types dates from the beginning of monasticism
in Egypt in the third century in such examples as St. Anthony
and St. Paul of Thebes. This type is commonly referred to as
the eremite, or hermit monk, who prefers to live alone in quiet.
The very name "monk" meaning "alone" (from the Greek
monos) indicates that ascetic life thrives on solitude. The second type is the semieremitical monk, initiated by St. Anthony
following twenty years of solitude. St. Anthony formally instituted monasticism as such by becoming the "father of monks,"
or their abbot. Thus a little colony of hermits were gathered
around him, exemplifying his ideals and sharing his ascetic
goal in concert with him. The monks, however, maintained
their individuality in community with one another. The third
type of monk is the cenobitic monk, or monk of the common
life. St. Pachomius and St. Basil in the fourth century and St.
Theodore the Studite in the eighth century are associated with
this monastic movement which sought to create a community
of monks who shared a common daily life. This is the most
prevalent type of monasticism in contemporary Orthodoxy
today.

The fourth and last type of monastic asceticism appeared on
Mt. Athos in the latter half of the fourteenth century during a
time of laxity in the practice of asceticism. This form of monastic life is known as idiorrhythmism. In essence, this monastic life enables the monks to acquire private property on
which to support themselves and thereby achieve independ-

ence from the abbot of the monastery whose authority and
weakness at times has been questioned. Idiorrhythmic monks
have instead set up a council to administer their own affairs.

Whatever form of monastic asceticism is followed, the over-
all impact has characterized Orthodoxy as a monastic tradition. For the non-Orthodox, monastic asceticism should not be
viewed solely as a harsh and grim way of existence with a mini-
mum of social utility (Chapter VII on church and state has
already indicated the social consciousness evident in monastic
life). In fact, the primary motive in the monastic community
is centered on love rather than self-denial. According to Abbot
Victory Matthew of the Monastery of the Transfiguration,
"Asceticism is a breathing into the heart of divine love, it is
the absorption of the loving soul by the Lord whom it loves."[14]
The underlying motivation for the monk is to attain purity of
heart. It is actually to this end that God gave man free will,
that he might choose to attain purity of heart whether in the
desert or in the crowded city. "If men withdraw from society
into the wilderness, it is not because they lack love: on the
contrary love is the very thing that drives them into solitude
—an all consuming love of God."[15] The monk's love finds
expression not only in deeds, but even more in praying for his
neighbor. The core of his life is prayer and contemplation
which nurture his love for God and man.

The monastic style of life is the stuff out of which saints are
born for the Kingdom of the Spirit. Monasticism points to the
eschatological significance of the Christian life. Monks seek
to live a heavenly life on earth. Herein lies the tension of their
lives between the "now" and the "not yet." Within this tension,
monasticism announces the Kingdom of the Spirit. Its presence
declares that the world has not yet come of age. Monasticism
contributes to both the East and the West precisely in remind-
ing us, immersed as we are in the world, that all our activities
come under God's judgment and mercy. The perennial temptation of Orthodox and non-Orthodox alike is to speak glibly of

the importance of the Spirit and then to proceed to forget its
role in our daily lives. Only as we look to the Kingdom of the
Spirit can the necessary interior and exterior cleansing take
place in us and in our respective churches in order that we
might truly give glory to God. Monasticism in today's secular
setting can serve as an important beacon amid the rapid cur-
rents tossing us in these revolutionary days. From monasticism
we can be reminded of our *eschaton* and take heart to advance
more boldly into the uncharted seas before us.

A Contemporary Ethic of Spirituality

While there is no doubt that monasticism has played an
important role in Christian history, the majority of Christians
will not consider their vocation in life to be monastic. To this
vast majority of Christians in all traditions the last section of
this chapter is devoted. Is there a contemporary ethic of spirituality, other than a monastic life, applicable to Orthodox,
Protestants, and Roman Catholics? Living within a post-Constantine (post-Christian) context of secularism, each Christian
tradition has been challenged to suggest guidelines rather than
rules that will enable Christians to be agents of reconciliation
rather than agents of rejection.[16] As we pursue a contemporary
ethic of spirituality the martyrs, monks, and saints of the past
will serve as valuable prototypes for our edification. No doubt
most of us will continue to be novices in the presence of a
martyr. Thus a contemporary ethic of spirituality will seek to
maintain continuity with the past while at the same time
remaining open to the future and to change.

Our goals for tomorrow call for an ecumenical *ethic of sociospirituality* to be begun today. The social and the spiritual
must be wedded as we confront life on this global island. The
social and the spiritual must be seen as a single unit of thought
and action, and all our strategy and budgetary planning must
maintain the creative balance necessary if our respective tradi-

tions are not to turn into self-contained ghettos, forsaking the
Lord of history who came into our midst for the sake of the
cosmos. The Christian's inner development and exterior pos-
ture are organically one. Pierre Teilhard de Chardin has
rightly described the threshold upon which we stand: "The
life of each one of us," he says, "is, as it were, woven of those
two threads: the thread of inward development, through
which our ideas and affections and our human and mystical
attitudes are gradually formed; and the thread of outward
success by which we always find ourselves at the exact point
at which the totality of the forces of the universe converge to
produce upon us the effect which God desires."[17] A contemporary ethic of spirituality can no longer seek the demonic luxury
of creating a dichotomy between spirituality and social concern. (Monasticism at its best has shown evidence of maintaining the closeness of the two.) The current situation in each of
our respective traditions indicates the harmful effects of polar-
ization between the spiritual and the social.

Development and practice of an ecumenical ethic of sociospirituality among Roman Catholics, Protestants, and Orthodox will further aid Faith and Order discussions. No doubt
such an ethic will save many a fruitless session from despair
and despondency as common action and prayer unite us where
our doctrinal statements continue to divide us. An ecumenical
ethic of sociospirituality will save us from a theological and
ecumenical standstill. We might refer to this ecumenical ethic
of sociospirituality as functional ecumenicism, more widely
known as "secular ecumenism." Such an ecumenical ethic
would be an outgrowth of a truly *Biblical ecumenism* encompassing the whole inhabited earth. A Biblical ecumenism will
seek to involve more than Christians in what can become a
worldwide ethic of sociospirituality. Total involvement of mankind cannot be overlooked, for each member of the human
society affects the other on our global island. The immensity
of this confrontation will be a major aspect of tomorrow's
dialogue for Christians.

Among Christians, an ecumenical ethic of sociospirituality must not attempt to escape the doctrinal and dogmatic formulations espoused by our respective traditions. Our ecumenism must be more than pragmatic; it must honestly seek truth. "Truth" admittedly is an evasive term, but personified in Christ it receives substantive form and content. An ecumenicity in quest of truth will by its very nature include theological implications. Like creeds and dogmas, ethical acts and behavior have always had a theological basis. Theological presuppositions are woven into our being and are a vital part of our style of life. An ecumenical ethic of sociospirituality as presently envisioned will have three basic theological presuppositions.

First, there must prevail a vivid sense of God's grace ministered to us through the Father, Son, and Spirit. The triune community of the Godhead is the provider of the grace we receive and experience as a gift. We are not passive recipients of God's gift but active partners who receive and translate his gracious gift into human expressions of mercy, love, acceptance, and aid. This dynamic view of God's grace should remind us once again that we are couriers of his grace, not creators of it. This initial point is fundamental to an adequate ecumenical ethic of sociospirituality.

Respective traditions among Christians will interpret this grace differently: Roman Catholics in categories of the supernatural, Orthodox as the process of deification (*theosis*), and Protestants as the undeserved, free action of God. Ecumenically valid for all these traditions, however, is the recognition that the founder of grace is God, not man. This important point of acknowledgment, namely, the givenness of grace, enables us to speak of grace as a gift and thus to agree on a God-centered rather than a man-centered orientation. The aim of Christian spirituality is to emphasize the truth that the source of our lives stems from the Triune God, not from ourselves. Without this constant awareness, our dimensions of social sensitivity would gradually diminish, replaced by egocentric and introverted concerns. Maintaining a clear focus that grace is a gift from God, that our very breathing at this moment is an experience of grace, will refresh and relax us as persons whose names are known to God and not as displaced, victimized, nameless digits in a "technopolis."

Disciplined spirituality nurtured by a lively sense of God's grace will actually equip us to reenter society with creative sensitivity to meet the needs of man, dependent upon God to supply and replenish our extended energies. Negligence of our praise and thanksgiving to God will weaken communications with our neighbor and his needs.

Second, in addition to the note of grace, an ecumenical ethic of sociospirituality should presuppose fortitude, to which Paul Tillich refers as the "courage to be." More specifically, one might say that a theology of grace must be accompanied by a *theology of courage.* Following the will of God and fulfilling the needs of man require courage. Words of grace lose their poignancy unless translated into concrete human deeds. Unless we dare to act upon the implications inherent in authentic piety, we have relegated ourselves to the pleasant enclosure within the sanctuary. The memorable history of civil rights demonstrations was a breakthrough from the musty ghetto to the smell and stink of the world. God has not one child but two—the child in the world as well as the child in the church— and it takes stamina and courage for either to look upon the other. The two children actually have need of each other.

Christian spirituality without social concern is a rejection of the incarnation, and social concern without spirituality lacks nurture. There should be an awareness of the dynamic relationship between God and the world. God, without diminishing his sovereignty, is in need of the world, and the world, without losing its freedom, is in need of God. Between them is a mystery known only to God. This mystery maintains a tension between our devotion to God and our response to our neighbor. Facing this tension requires courage; attempting to witness creatively requires grace.

The third presupposition for an ecumenical ethic of socio-spirituality is a renewed affirmation by all Christians of the material in life. Orthodox Christians may contribute greatly to us in the West at this point. The East has shown more concern for the role of matter in its theologizing than has the West with its tendency to spiritualize material needs away. It seems essential for a sound ethic of sociospirituality that the West as well as the East once again affirm the material along with the spiritual well-being of persons. In addition to the theology of grace and courage, it is necessary that we advocate a positive *theology of goods*. An affirmation of goods, consisting of the varied items produced and consumed by a techno-cratic society, completes the list of presuppositions underlying a contemporary ethic of sociospirituality that would be ecumenically valid for all Christians.

The late Pope John XXIII's encyclical *Pacem in Terris*, hailed by Roman Catholics and many others, was a creative expression approximating closely what is implied by a theology of goods. The more recent encyclical by Pope Paul VI, *Populorum Progressio*, further fortifies Pope John's statement. Christian spirituality, listening to the world in which it finds itself, will avoid the pitfalls inherent in Gnostic-Manichaean forms of piety which devaluate the material in life. If spirituality is defined and understood as sensitivity and desire to do the will of God in meeting the needs of our fellowmen, then a theology of goods will of necessity be one of the pillars implicit within an ecumenical ethic of sociospirituality.

So much of our worship is irrelevant precisely at this junc-ture; man's physical needs have been ignored or minimized. Communism is actually a heretical perversion of a theology of goods without grace. Communism affirms the material but denies the Creator of the material. Christianity can rectify the situation by establishing the proper balance between goods and grace, by a fresh look at the incarnate Word become flesh. Jesus Christ is the Man who dared to die for the well-being of others. His coming in flesh is a manifestation of the Creator's concern for man's material as well as spiritual welfare. A theology of goods points to a Christian materialism, which calls for integrity and wisdom in the use of God's creation.

Grace, courage, and goods, then, are the vital presuppositions supporting a contemporary ethic of sociospirituality. A common spirituality that is socially sensitive toward God and neighbor will advance, not retard, our search for renewal among the apparently insoluble doctrinal issues that separate the household of Christians. Cooperative endeavors can serve as a thirst-refreshing oasis in our important encounters in the realm of Faith and Order. And more immediately, churchmen in our respective traditions by drawing together in areas of common concern will remove stereotypes of each other and discover the authenticity of each other's Christian heritage in a way hitherto largely unrealized.

Selected Bibliography

Full details of all other works cited (including journals) are given in the appropriate footnotes.

Abbott, Walter M. (ed.), *The Documents of Vatican II.* The America Press, 1966.

Anderson, Gerald H. (ed.), *The Theology of the Christian Mission.* McGraw-Hill Book Company, Inc., 1961.

Arseniev, Nicholas, *Russian Piety,* tr. by Asheleigh Moorhouse. London: The Faith Press, 1964.

Attwater, Donald (ed.), *The Christian Churches of the East,* 2 vols. London: Geoffrey Chapman, Ltd., Publishers, 1961.

Baillie, Donald M., and Marsh, John (eds.), *Intercommunion.* Harper & Brothers, 1952.

Barker, Ernest (ed. and tr.), *Social and Political Thought in Byzantium.* Oxford: Clarendon Press, 1957.

Barth, Karl, *Church Dogmatics,* Vols. I and IV, ed. by G. W. Bromiley and T. F. Torrance. Edinburgh: T. & T. Clark, 1936 ff.

————— *The Humanity of God.* John Knox Press, 1960.

Bartsch, Hans Werner (ed.), *Kerygma and Myth: A Theological Debate.* Harper Torchbooks, The Cloister Library, Harper & Brothers, 1961.

Baynes, N. H., and Moss, H. St. L. B. (eds.), *Byzantium: An Introduction to East Roman Civilization.* Oxford: Clarendon Press, 1962.

Bea, Augustin Cardinal, *The Unity of Christians,* ed. by Bernard Leeming. Herder & Herder, Inc., 1963.

Bennett, John C. (ed.), *Christian Social Ethics in a Changing World*. Association Press, 1966.

Benz, Ernst, *The Eastern Orthodox Church: Its Thought and Life*. Doubleday & Company, Inc., 1963.

——— *Die Ostkirche im Lichte der Protestantischen Geschichtsschreibung von der Reformation bis zur Gegenwart*. Freibourg: Verlag Karl Alber, 1952.

———*Russische Heiligenlegenden*. Zurich: Verlag Die Waage, 1953.

——— *Wittenberg und Byzanz*. Marburg: Elwert-Grafe und Unzer Verlag, 1949.

Berdyaev, Nicolas, *Spirit and Reality*. London: The Centenary Press, 1946.

Biot, François, *The Rise of Protestant Monasticism*, tr. by W. J. Kerrigan. Helicon Press, Inc., 1963.

Birbeck, W. J., *Russia and the English Church* (new edition). London: S. P. C. K., 1948.

Blake, Eugene Carson, *The Church in the Next Decade*. The Macmillan Company, 1966.

Bogolepov, Alexander A., *Orthodox Hymns*. Russian Orthodox Theological Fund, Inc., 1965.

——— *Toward an American Orthodox Church: The Establishment of an Autocephalous Orthodox Church*. Morehouse-Barlow Co., 1963.

Bolshakoff, Serge, *The Doctrine of the Unity of the Church in the Works of Khomyakov and Moehler*. London: S. P. C. K., 1946.

Bourdeaux, Michael, *Opium of the People: The Christian Religion in the U.S.S.R.* The Bobbs-Merrill Company, Inc., 1966.

Bridston, Keith R., and Wagoner, W. D. (eds.), *Unity in Mid-Career: An Ecumenical Critique*. The Macmillan Company, 1963.

Brightman, F. E., *Liturgies: Eastern and Western*, Vol. I. Oxford: Clarendon Press, 1896.

Bulgakov, Sergius, *The Orthodox Church*. London: The Centenary Press, 1935.

Calian, C. S., *Berdyaev's Philosophy of Hope*. Augsburg Publishing House, 1969.

—————— *The Significance of Echatology in the Thoughts of Nicolas Berdyaev*. Leiden: E. J. Brill, 1965.

Callahan, Daniel J., Obermann, H. A., and O'Hanlon, D. J. (eds.), *Christianity Divided*. Sheed & Ward, Inc., 1961.

Calvin, John, *Calvin: Institutes of the Christian Religion*, ed. by John T. McNeill, tr. and indexed by Ford Lewis Battles (The Library of Christian Classics, Vols. XXI–XXII). The Westminster Press, 1960.

Campenhausen, Hans von, *The Fathers of the Greek Church*, tr. by L. A. Garrard. London: Adam & Charles Black, Ltd., 1963.

—————— *The Virgin Birth in the Theology of the Ancient Church*. London: SCM Press, Ltd., 1964.

Cavarnos, Constantine (ed.), *Byzantine Sacred Music*. Institute for Byzantine and Modern Greek Studies, 1956.

Chadwick, Henry, *Early Christian Thought and the Classical Tradition*. Oxford University Press, 1966.

Cochrane, Arthur C. (ed.), *Reformed Confessions of the 16th Century*. The Westminster Press, 1966.

Coleman, Christopher B., *Constantine the Great and Christianity*. Columbia University Press, 1914.

Come, Arnold B., *Agents of Reconciliation* (rev. and enlarged ed.). The Westminster Press, 1964.

Congar, Yves, *After Nine Hundred Years: The Background of the Schism Between the Eastern and the Western Churches*. Fordham University Press, 1959.

—————— *Lay People in the Church: A Study for a Theology of the Laity*, tr. by Donald Attwater. The Newman Press, 1957.

Constantelos, Demetrios J., *Byzantine Philanthropy and Social Welfare*. Rutgers University Press, 1966.

—————— *The Greek Orthodox Church: Faith, History, and Practice*. The Seabury Press, Inc., 1967.

Cragg, Kenneth, *The Call of the Minaret*. Oxford University Press, 1956.

Cullmann, Oscar, *The Early Church: Studies in Early Christian History and Theology*, tr. by A. J. B. Higgins and S. Godman. The Westminster Press, 1956.

—————— *The State in the New Testament*. London: SCM Press, Ltd., 1957.

Dewart, Leslie, *The Future of Belief: Theism in a World Come of Age.* Herder & Herder, Inc., 1966.

Dix, Gregory, *The Shape of the Liturgy.* Westminster, London: The Dacre Press, 1946.

Downey, G., *Constantinople in the Days of Justinian.* University of Oklahoma, 1960.

Dvornik, Francis, *Byzantium and the Roman Primacy.* Fordham University Press, 1966.

——— *The Ecumenical Councils.* Hawthorn Books, Inc., Publishers, 1961.

——— *The Photian Schism: History and Legend.* Cambridge: Cambridge University Press, 1948.

Eastwood, Cyril, *The Royal Priesthood of the Faithful.* Augsburg Publishing House, 1963.

Edwall, Pehr, *et al.* (eds.), *Ways of Worship: The Report of a Theological Commission of Faith and Order.* Harper & Brothers, 1951.

Englert, Clement C., *Catholics and Orthodox—Can They Unite?* The Paulist Press, 1961.

Evdokimov, Paul, *L'Orthodoxie.* Paris: Editions Delachaux et Niestlé, 1965.

——— *The Struggle with God,* tr. by Sister Gertrude. The Paulist Press, 1966.

Every, George, *The Byzantine Patriarchate, 451–1204* (2d ed. rev.). London: S. P. C. K., 1962.

——— *Misunderstandings Between East and West.* John Knox Press, 1966.

Farley, Edward, *Requiem for a Lost Piety: The Contemporary Search for the Christian Life.* The Westminster Press, 1966.

Fedotov, G. P., *The Russian Religious Mind,* 2 vols. Harper & Brothers, 1960; Harvard University Press, 1966.

——— (ed.), *A Treasury of Russian Spirituality.* Harper & Row, Publishers, Inc., 1965.

Fletcher, William C., *A Study in Survival.* The Macmillan Company, 1965.

French, R. M., *The Eastern Orthodox Church.* London: Hutchinson University Library, 1961.

Fry, E. L. B., and Armstrong, A. H. (eds.), *Rediscovering*

Eastern Christendom. London: Darton, Longman & Todd, Ltd., 1963.

Geanakoplos, Deno John, *Byzantine East and Latin West: Two Worlds of Christendom in Middle Ages and Renaissance.* Harper Torchbooks, The Academy Library, Harper & Row, Publishers, Inc., 1966.

Germanos, Metropolitan of Thyateira, *Kyrillos Loukaris 1572–1638: A Struggle for Preponderance Between Catholic and Protestant Powers in the Orthodox East.* London: S. P. C. K., 1951.

Gill, Joseph, *The Council of Florence.* Cambridge: Cambridge University Press, 1959.

———— *Personalities of the Council of Florence.* Barnes & Noble, Inc., 1964.

Glazik, Josef, *Die Islammission der Russisch Orthodoxen Kirche.* Münster: 1959.

———— *Die Russische-Orthodoxe Heidenmission seit Peter dem Grossen.* Münster: Aschendorffsche Verlagsbuchhandlung, 1954.

Greenslade, S. L., *Church and State from Constantine to Theodosius.* London: SCM Press, Ltd., 1954.

———— *Schism in the Early Church.* London: SCM Press, Ltd., 1964.

Hadjiantoniou, George A., *Protestant Patriarch: The Life of Cyril Lucaris (1572–1638) Patriarch of Constantinople.* John Knox Press, 1961.

Haroutunian, Joseph, *God with Us: A Theology of Transpersonal Life.* The Westminster Press, 1965.

Heijke, John, *An Ecumenical Light on the Renewal of Religious Community Life: Taizé.* Duquesne University Press, 1967.

Heiler, Friedrich, *Urkirche und Ostkirche.* Munich: Von Ernst Reinhardt, 1937.

Istavridis, Vasil T., *Historia tes Oikoumenikes Kineseos.* Athens, 1964.

———— *Orthodoxia kai Anglikanismos.* Athens, 1963.

Iswolsky, Hélène, *Christ in Russia: The Historic Tradition and Life of the Russian Church.* Bruce Publishing Company, 1960.

Jedin, Hubert, *Ecumenical Councils of the Catholic Church,* tr. by Ernest Graf. Herder & Herder, Inc., 1960.

—— *A History of the Council of Trent,* tr. by Ernest Graf, Vol. I. B. Herder Book Company, 1957.

Jurji, Edward J. (ed.) *The Ecumenical Era in Church and Society.* The Macmillan Company, 1959.

Kadloubovsky, E., and Palmer, G. E. N. (eds. and trs.), *Early Fathers from the Philokalia.* London: Faber & Faber, Ltd., 1953.

Karmiris, J. N., *Orthodoxia kai Protestantismos.* Athens, 1937.

Kelly, J. N. D., *Early Christian Creeds.* London: Longmans, Green & Co., Ltd. 1960.

—— *Early Christian Doctrines,* 2d ed. Harper & Brothers, 1960.

Khomiakov, Alexis S., *The Church Is One,* with an Introduction by Nicolas Zernov. London: S. P. C. K., 1948.

Kondakov, Nikodim P., *The Russian Icon.* Oxford: Clarendon Press, 1927.

Kontoglous, Photēs, *Byzantine Sacred Art: Selected Writings of the Contemporary Greek Icon Painter According to the Tradition of Eastern Orthodox Christianity,* compiled, tr., and ed. by Constantine Cavarnos. Vantage Press, Inc., 1957.

Korper, Ruth, *The Candlelight Kingdom.* The Macmillan Company, 1955.

Kraemer, Hendrik, *A Theology of the Laity.* The Westminster Press, 1958.

Kung, Hans, *The Council and Reform.* Sheed & Ward, Inc., 1961.

—— *Structures of the Church.* Thomas Nelson & Sons, 1964.

Leeming, Bernard, *The Vatican Council and Christian Unity.* Harper & Row, Publishers, Inc., 1966.

Le Guillou, M. J., *The Spirit of Eastern Orthodoxy.* Hawthorne Books, Inc., Publishers, 1962.

Lehmann, Paul, *Ethics in a Christian Context.* Harper & Row, Publishers, Inc., 1963.

Leith, John (ed.), *Creeds of Christendom.* Doubleday & Company, Inc., 1963.

Lieb, Fritz, *Sophia und Historie.* Zurich: EVZ-Verlag, 1962.

Lossky, Vladimir, *The Mystical Theology of the Eastern*

Church, tr. by the Fellowship of St. Alban and St. Sergius. London: James Clarke & Company, Ltd., Publishers, 1957.

McCrea, Samuel, *On the Road to Unity.* Harper & Brothers, 1961.

MacGregor, Geddes, *Corpus Christi: The Nature of the Church According to the Reformed Tradition.* The Westminster Press, 1958.

Mackay, John A. *Ecumenics: The Science of the Church Universal.* Prentice-Hall, Inc., 1964.

McKenzie, John L., *Authority in the Church.* Sheed & Ward, Inc., 1966.

Mackie, Robert C., and West, Charles C. (eds.), *The Sufficiency of God: Essays on the Ecumenical Hope in Honor of W. A. Visser 't Hooft.* The Westminster Press, 1963.

McLuhan, Marshall, *Understanding Media: The Extensions of Man.* McGraw-Hill Book Company, Inc., 1964.

McNeill, John T., *Unitive Protestantism.* John Knox Press, 1964.

Manson, T. W., *Ministry and Priesthood: Christ's and Ours.* London, The Epworth Press, Publishers, 1958.

Margull, Hans J. (ed.), *The Councils of the Church: History and Analysis,* tr. by Walter F. Bense. Fortress Press, 1966.

Mascall, Eric L. (ed.), *The Church of God.* London: S.P.C.K., 1934.

———— *The Mother of God.* Westminster, London: The Dacre Press, 1959.

Matossian, Mary A. K., *The Impact of Soviet Policies in Armenia.* Leiden: E. J. Brill, 1962.

Meyendorff, John, *The Orthodox Church.* Pantheon Books, Inc., 1962.

———— *Orthodoxy and Catholicity.* Sheed & Ward, Inc., 1966.

———— *A Study of Gregory Palamas.* London: The Faith Press, 1964.

———— *et al. The Primacy of Peter.* London: The Faith Press, 1963.

Moehler, John A., *Symbolism.* Edward Dungian, 1844.

A Monk of the Eastern Church, *Orthodox Spirituality.* London: S. P. C. K., 1957.

Mudge, Lewis S., *One Church: Catholic and Reformed.* The Westminster Press, 1963.

Muller, Ludolf, *Die Kritik des Protestantismus in der russischen Theologie vom 16. bis zum 18. Jahrhundert.* Wiesbaden, 1951.

——— *Solovjev und der Protestantismus.* Freibourg: Herder & Co., 1951.

Neill, Stephen C., and Weber, Hans-Ruedi (eds.), *The Layman in Christian History.* The Westminster Press, 1963.

Niesel, Wilhelm, *The Gospel and the Churches: A Comparison of Catholicism, Orthodoxy, and Protestantism,* tr. by David Lewis. The Westminster Press, 1962.

——— *The Theology of Calvin.* The Westminster Press, 1956.

O'Meara, Thomas A., *Mary in Protestant and Catholic Theology.* Sheed & Ward, Inc., 1966.

Ouspensky, Leonide, and Lossky, Vladimir, *The Meaning of Icons.* Switzerland: Otto Walter, Ltd., 1952.

Pelikan, Jaroslav, *The Finality of Jesus Christ in an Age of Universal History—A Dilemma of the Third Century.* John Knox Press, 1966.

——— *The Light of the World.* Harper & Brothers, 1962.

——— *The Shape of Death.* Abingdon Press, 1961.

——— (ed.), *The Preaching of Chrysostom.* Fortress Press, 1967.

Philippou, A. J. (ed.), *The Orthodox Ethos.* Oxford: Holywell Press, 1964.

Pittenger, Norman W., *The Church, the Ministry, and Reunion.* The Seabury Press, Inc., 1957.

Prestige, G. L., *God in Patristic Thought.* London: S.P.C.K., 1964.

Rahner, Karl, *Bishops: Their Status and Function.* Helicon Press, Inc., 1963.

Reid, J. K. S., *The Biblical Doctrine of the Ministry.* London: Oliver & Boyd, Ltd., 1955.

Riha, Thomas (ed.), *Readings in Russian Civilization,* Vol. I. The University of Chicago Press, 1964.

Riley, Athelstan (ed.), *Birbeck and the Russian Church.* The Macmillan Company, 1917.

Selected Bibliography   179

Ritschl, Dietrich, *Athanasius* (Theologische Studien, Heft 76). Zurich: EVZ-Verlag, 1964.
Robinson, J. M., and Cobb, J. B., Jr. (eds.), *The New Hermeneutic*. Harper & Row, Publishers, Inc., 1964.
Robinson, N. F., *Monasticism in the Orthodox Church*. London: Cope & Fenwick, 1964.
Rouse, Ruth, and Neil, Stephen Charles (eds.), *A History of the Ecumenical Movement, 1517–1948*. The Westminster Press, 1954.
Runciman, Steven, *Byzantine Civilization*. London: Edward Arnold (Publishers), Ltd., 1959.
——— *The Eastern Schism*. Oxford: Clarendon Press, 1956.
Salville, S., *An Introduction to the Study of Eastern Liturgies*. London: Sands & Co. (Publishers), Ltd., 1938.
Sarkissian, Karekin, *The Council of Chalcedon and the Armenian Church*. London: S.P.C.K., 1965.
Sarxian, Vardan, *Sacred Music of the Armenian Church*, 2 vols. Armenian Choir Association, 1967.
Sayegh, Maximos IV, Patriarch of Antioch (ed.), *The Eastern Churches and Catholic Unity*, tr. by John Dingle *et al*. Herder & Herder, Inc., 1963.
Schlier, R., *Der Patriarch Kyrill Lukaris von Konstantinopel*. Marburg, 1927.
Schmemann, Alexander, *The Historical Road of Eastern Orthodoxy*. Holt, Rinehart and Winston, Inc., 1963.
——— *Introduction to Liturgical Theology*. London: The Faith Press, 1966.
——— *Sacraments and Orthodoxy*. Herder & Herder, Inc., 1965.
Schutz, Roger, *Living Today for God*. Helicon Press, Inc., 1962.
Schweizer, Eduard, *Church Order in the New Testament*, tr. by Frank Clarke. London: SCM Press, Ltd., 1961.
Sellers, Robert V., *The Council of Chalcedon: A Historical and Doctrinal Survey*. London: S. P. C. K., 1953.
Shaw, P. E., *American Contacts with the Eastern Churches, 1820–1870*. American Society of Church History, 1937.
——— *The Early Tractarians and the Eastern Church*. Morehouse-Gorham Company, 1930.

Shepherd, M. H., Jr., *The Reform of Liturgical Worship*. Oxford University Press, 1961.

—— (ed.), *Worship in Scripture and Tradition*. Oxford University Press, 1963.

Sherrard, Philip, *Athos: The Mountain of Silence*. London: Oxford University Press, 1960.

—— *The Greek East and the Latin West*. Oxford University Press, 1959.

Slenczka, Reinhard, *Ostkirche und Okumene*. Göttingen: Vandenhoeck & Ruprecht, 1962.

Smith, Elwyn A., *Church-State Relations in Ecumenical Perspective*. Duquesne University Press, 1966.

Soloviev, Vladimir, *Russia and the Universal Church*, tr. by Herbert Rees. London: Geoffrey Bles, Ltd., 1948.

—— *War, Progress and the End of History: Including a Short Story of the Antichrist*. London: University Press, 1915.

Stevenson, J. (ed.), *Creeds, Councils and Controversies*. The Seabury Press, Inc., 1966.

Struve, Nikita, *Christians in Contemporary Russia*, tr. by Lancelot Sheppard and A. Mason. Charles Scribner's Sons, 1967.

Teilhard de Chardin, Pierre, *The Divine Milieu*. Harper & Brothers, 1960.

Thunberg, Lars, *Microcosm and Mediator: The Theological Anthropology of Maximus the Confessor*. Lund: C. W. K. Gleerup, Publishers, 1965.

Thurian, Max, *Consecration of the Layman*. Helicon Press, Inc., 1963.

—— *Mary: Mother of the Lord, Figure of the Church*. London: The Faith Press, 1962.

—— *Modern Man and Spiritual Life*. Association Press, 1963.

—— *Visible Unity and Tradition*. London: Darton, Longman & Todd, Ltd., 1964.

Todd, John M. (ed.), *Problems of Authority*. Helicon Press, Inc., 1962.

Torrance, T. F., *Theology in Reconstruction*. Wm. B. Eerdmans Publishing Company, 1965.

The United Presbyterian Church in the U.S.A., *Book of Confessions*. Office of the General Assembly of The United Presbyterian Church in the U.S.A., 1967.

Vahanian, Gabriel, *No Other God*. George Braziller, Inc., 1966.

Vassady, Bela, *Christ's Church: Evangelical, Catholic and Reformed*. Wm. B. Eerdmans Publishing Company, 1964.

Verghese, Paul, *The Joy of Freedom: Eastern Worship and Modern Man*. London: Lutterworth Press, 1967.

Visser 't Hooft, W. A., *Anglo-Catholicism and Orthodoxy—A Protestant View*. London: SCM Press, Ltd., 1933.

———— *The Meaning of Ecumenical*. London: SCM Press, Ltd., 1953.

Waddams, Herbert (ed.), *Anglo-Russian Theological Conference*. London: The Faith Press, 1957.

Waddell, Helen, *The Desert Fathers*. University of Michigan Press, 1960.

Ware, Timothy, *Eustratios Argenti—A Study of the Greek Church Under Turkish Rule*. Oxford: Clarendon Press, 1964.

———— *The Orthodox Church*. Penguin Books, Inc., 1963.

Welch, Claude, *In This Name*. Charles Scribner's Sons, 1952.

———— *The Reality of the Church*. Charles Scribner's Sons, 1958.

World Student Christian Federation (ed.), *History Lessons for Tomorrow's Mission*. Geneva: WSCF, 1960.

Zander, L. A., *Vision and Action*. London: Victor Gollancz, Ltd., 1952.

Zernov, Nicolas, *Eastern Christendom*. London: Weidenfeld and Nicolson, 1961.

———— *Orthodox Encounter*. London: James Clarke & Company, Ltd., Publishers, 1961.

Notes

Chapter I.
A SHORT HISTORY OF ORTHODOX-PROTESTANT RELATIONS

1. Georges Florovsky, "The Orthodox Churches and the Ecumenical Movement Prior to 1910," *A History of the Ecumenical Movement, 1517–1948*, ed. by Ruth Rouse and Stephen Charles Neill, p. 176.

2. Georges Florovsky, "An Early Ecumenical Correspondence" (Patriarch Jeremiah II and the Lutheran Divines), *World Lutheranism of Today* (Stockholm: Svenska Kyrkans Diakonistryreles Bokforlag, 1950), p. 103.

3. *Ibid.*, pp. 103–104.

4. *Ibid.*, p. 100.

5. *Ibid.*, pp. 100–101. It should be added that another notable event involved the desire of the Lutherans to put the Bible into the hands of Orthodox believers. Through meetings between Orthodox Prince Constantine Ostrogsky and Lutherans (including Calvinists and Brethren ministers) the first Slavonic Bible was printed in Ostrog in Volhynia in 1580. This can be interpreted as one of the earliest ecumenical enterprises successfully undertaken by Orthodox and Protestants. (Florovsky, "The Orthodox Churches and the Ecumenical Movement," in Rouse and Neill [eds.], *Ecumenical Movement*, p. 182.)

6. Florovsky, "An Early Ecumenical Correspondence," *World Lutheranism of Today*, p. 99.

7. George A. Hadjiantoniou, *Protestant Patriarch: The Life of Cyril Lucaris (1572–1638) Patriarch of Constantinople*. The

appendix of his volume includes an English translation of
Cyril's "Eastern Confession of the Christian Faith."

8. In addition to Hadjiantoniou, works on Cyril by Benz,
Germanos, and Schlier are listed in the Bibliography.

9. Florovsky, "The Orthodox Churches and the Ecumenical
Movement," in Rouse and Neill (eds.), *Ecumenical Movement*, p. 185.

10. *Ibid.*, p. 185. Orthodox theologian J. N. Karmiris (see
Orthodoxia kai Protestantismos) points out that only three of
the total eighteen chapters of the *Confession* are fully Orthodox in teaching. Lucaris in his *Confession* followed the Calvinist doctrine of predestination and election; the witness of
Scripture was ranked as higher authority than the church itself—in other words belief in the infallibility of the church was
denied, and the invisible aspects of the church were stressed
over its visible features. He rejected the veneration of icons,
and believed in only two rather than seven sacraments. Finally,
he rejected any doctrine of transubstantiation (*metousiosis*)
and emphasized instead the presence in the Eucharist of Christ
which faith enables us to receive and experience. (Timothy
Ware, *Eustratios Argenti—A Study of the Greek Church Under Turkish Rule*, pp. 8–9.) There is little doubt as to why the
Orthodox were upset by Lucaris.

11. Ware, *Eustratios Argenti*, p. 11.

12. John Meyendorff, "The Significance of the Reformation
in the History of Christendom," *The Ecumenical Review*, Vol.
XVI, No. 2 (1964), p. 176. Meyendorff adds, "So an encounter
took place, but how much of a dialogue? Neither the historical
circumstances nor the theological climate permitted more than
a mutual understanding" (*ibid.*). However, it should be pointed
out to Meyendorff that there were exceptions, though admittedly isolated cases. For example, the Dutch Reformed theologian Hugo Grotius (1583–1645) truly tried to cultivate the
attitude for proper dialogue, not desirous of absorbing Orthodoxy into Protestantism but seeking equality for all the
churches as they reach out for the authentic dimensions of catholicity. (Martin Schmidt, "Ecumenical Activity on the Con-
tinent of Europe in the Seventeenth and Eighteenth Centu-

ries," in Rouse and Neill [eds.], *Ecumenical Movement,* p. 94.)

13. Ware, *Eustratios Argenti,* pp. 8–9.

14. *Ibid.,* p. 11. "The Latinizing tendency is found most notably in two other seventeenth century Confessions, both intended as an answer to Loukaris, the one by Peter of Moghila, Metropolitan of Kiev from 1633 to 1647, the other by Dositheos, Patriarch of Jerusalem from 1669 to 1707. But although under Latin influence, Peter and Dositheos deviated at some points from the main stream of Orthodox tradition, their deviation is far less radical than that of Cyril. . . . *The Orthodox Confession* of Moghila represents the high-water mark of Latin influence upon Orthodox theology, for although Latinisms are also apparent in the Confession of Dositheos, they are less serious." (*Ibid.,* pp. 11, 13.)

15. Florovsky's term ("The Orthodox Churches and the Ecumenical Movement" in Rouse and Neill [eds.], *Ecumenical Movement,* p. 186).

16. For example, "Theophanes Prokopovich (1681–1736) had studied in the Jesuit College in Rome, and had actually become a Roman Catholic. However, on returning to Kiev in 1704, he resumed his Orthodox faith, and became professor of theology and later rector of the theological academy in that place. In 1718 he was appointed Bishop of Pskov by Peter the Great. By reaction against Roman Catholicism, he introduced a number of Protestant theological text-books into the course of studies, and his own System of Theology, written in Latin, was in the main based on the *Syntagma* of Amand Polanus, a Reformed theologian of Basle. The successors of Prokopovich followed his lead" (*ibid.*). Compare with Eustratios Argenti of Chios (1687–1757), a Greek theologian of this period, whose works though polemical have retained the spirit of Orthodox thought. (See Ware, *Eustratios Argenti.*)

17. Florovsky, "The Orthodox Churches and the Ecumenical Movement," in Rouse and Neill (eds.), *Ecumenical Movement,* p. 189.

18. See Chapter VII for further explanation of church-state relations in the Byzantine Church.

19. Florovsky, "The Orthodox Churches and the Ecumeni-

cal Movement" in Rouse and Neill (eds.), *Ecumenical Movement*, p. 189.

20. *Ibid.* The booklet was produced by foreign scholars who had studied at the Academy of Science at St. Petersburg. Cf. J. P. Kohlius, *Ecclesia graeca lutheranizans; sive exercitatio de consensu ac dissensu orientalis graecae, speciatim russicae, et occidentalis lutheranae ecclesiae in dogmatibus* (Lubeck, 1723).

21. Florovsky, "The Orthodox Churches and the Ecumenical Movement" in Rouse and Neill (eds.), *Ecumenical Movement*, p. 189.

22. *Ibid.*, pp. 161–164.

23. The concordat was signed in London on August 18, 1716, and sent to the Russian czar, Peter the Great, who forwarded it on to the Eastern Patriarchs (*ibid.*, p. 192).

24. *Ibid.*

25. *Ibid.*, p. 193.

26. First published in 1864 in Russian, in *Pravoslanoe Obozrenie* (*The Orthodox Review*), and again in the second volume of *Khomiakov's Works* (Prague, 1867).

27. Georges Florovsky, "Orthodox Ecumenism in the 19th Century," *St. Vladimir's Seminary Quarterly*, Spring-Summer, 1956, pp. 1–54. An abridged account is found in Rouse and Neill (eds.), *Ecumenical Movement*, pp. 193–215.

28. Cf. Judith Cohen Zacek, "The Russian Bible Society and the Russian Orthodox Church," *Church History*, Vol. 35 (December, 1966), pp. 411–437.

29. Florovsky, "Orthodox Ecumenism," *loc. cit.*, p. 7.

30. *Ibid.*, p. 21. Khomiakov continued, "The Church cannot be a harmony of discords; it cannot be a numerical sum of Orthodox, Latins, and Protestants. It is nothing if it is not perfect inward harmony of creed and outward harmony of expression" (*ibid.*, taken from Khomiakov, *L'Eglise Latine et Protestantisme au point de vue de l'Eglise d'Orient;* Lausanne et Vevey, 1872).

31. For further understanding of the Tractarian movement, see P. E. Shaw, *The Early Tractarians and the Eastern Church*.

32. Florovsky, "Orthodox Ecumenism," *loc. cit.*, p. 7.

33. *Ibid.*, p. 32. Guettée later influenced Eugene Michaud,

who in turn stimulated the Old Catholic Church to seek relations with Orthodoxy (*ibid.*, pp. 30–32).

34. *Ibid.*, pp. 47–49; Rouse and Neill (eds.), *Ecumenical
Movement*, pp. 662–663.

35. *Ibid.*, p. 27.

36. *Ibid.*, p. 52

37. *Ibid.*

38. Listed in Bibliography.

39. Meyendorff, "The Significance of the Reformation," *loc.
cit.*, p. 179.

40. A new translation of the 1920 message of the Ecumenical
Patriarchate can be found in *The Ecumenical Review*, Vol. XII
(1959–1960), pp. 79–82.

41. Keith R. Bridston and W. D. Wagoner (eds.), *Unity in
Mid-Career: An Ecumenical Critique*, p. 56.

Chapter II.
THE GREEK PATRISTIC TRADITION: A COMMON HERITAGE

1. John T. McNeill writes briefly on John Calvin's use of the
church fathers, "Calvin as an Ecumenical Churchman," *Church
History*, Vol. 32 (1963), pp. 379–391. More research is needed
to discover the insights gained by the Reformers from the
church fathers.

2. The terms "East" and "West" are used here not simply as
topographical or ethnographical designations. These labels
represent theological principles and attitudes, not merely geographic territories.

3. Editorial report in *The Christian Century*, August 14,
1963.

4. Father Georges Florovsky believes that the East best
maintains the patristic mentality and attitude, "The Eastern
Orthodox Church and the Ecumenical Movement," *Theology
Today*, Vol. 7 (1950–1951), p. 73.

5. A patristics study group sponsored by the World Council
of Churches' Faith and Order Commission is currently studying St. Basil the Great's view of the Holy Spirit. While such a
study group is commendable, the weight of Blake's comment is
that the World Council of Churches theologically and prac-

tically today reflects primarily Western thought, with only a token assent to Eastern thought.

6. Florovsky, "The Eastern Orthodox Church," *loc. cit.*, p. 71.

7. George Huntston Williams, "Georges Vasilievich Florovsky: His American Career (1948–1965)," *The Greek Orthodox Theological Review*, Vol. XI, No. 1 (Summer, 1965), pp. 56–57.

8. Georges Florovsky, "Saint Gregory Palamas and the Tradition of the Fathers," *Sobornost'*, Winter-Spring, 1961, p. 167.

9. Cf. Philip Sherrard, *The Greek East and the Latin West*.

10. Florovsky, "Saint Gregory Palamas," *loc. cit.*, p. 180. See also John Romanides, "Highlights in the Debate Over Theodore of Mopsuestia's Christology," *The Greek Orthodox Theological Review*, Vol. 5 (1959–1960), pp. 140–185.

11. Florovsky, "Saint Gregory Palamas," *loc. cit.*, p. 180.

12. Some Orthodox contend that there is too great an emphasis on the first five centuries as the Greek patristic period. From such a stance, periodization can and has led in some quarters of Orthodoxy to a static understanding of antiquity. Father Florovsky argues that "after all, it does not make much difference, whether we *restrict* the normative authority of the Church to one century, or to five, or to eight. *There should be no restriction at all*" ("Saint Gregory Palamas," *loc. cit.*, p. 170).

13. See Henry Chadwick, *Early Christian Thought and the Classical Tradition*.

14. See the discussion in "The Theologian and the Philosopher: A Dialogue," *Religion in Life*, Summer, 1964.

15. Hans von Campenhausen, *The Fathers of the Greek Church*, p. 8.

16. Chadwick, *Early Christian Thought*, p. 17.

17. *Ibid.*, p. 19.

18. Oscar Cullmann, *The Early Church*. Note especially the chapter on "The Tradition."

19. Chadwick, *Early Christian Thought*, p. 39 (original found in *Protrepticus* 95).

20. *Ibid.*, p. 44 (original found in *Stromateis* VI. 66).

21. *Ibid.*, p. 50 (original found in *Stromateis* VI. 52).

22. *Ibid.*, p. 59 (original from *Stromateis* III. 105 and 82).

23. I find a kinship of attitude between Origen and the cele-brated Episcopal bishops John A. T. Robinson and James Pike.

24. *Commentary in Genesis,* cited in the Preface to Pam-philus' *Apology* (XXIV. 296, Lommatzsch), found in Chad-wick, *Early Christian Thought,* p. 123.

25. Jaroslav Pelikan, *The Finality of Jesus Christ in an Age of Universal History—A Dilemma of the Third Century.* See also World Council of Churches, *Bulletin,* Division of Studies, VIII–2 (Autumn, 1962).

26. Pelikan, *The Finality of Jesus Christ,* p. 51.

27. *Ibid.,* p. 52

28. Von Campenhausen, *The Fathers of the Greek Church,* p. 69. See also Dietrich Ritschl, *Athanasius* (Theologische Stu-dien, Heft 76).

29. Von Campenhausen, *The Fathers of the Greek Church,* p. 72.

30. Jaroslav Pelikan, *The Light of the World,* p. 77.

31. Cf. Georges Florovsky, "The Concept of Creation in Saint Athanasius," *Studia Patristica,* Vol. VI (1962), pp. 26–77.

32. Von Campenhausen, *The Fathers of the Greek Church,* p. 93. The Trinity will be discussed in Chapter X.

33. See the reports of the World Alliance of Reformed and Presbyterian Churches at its nineteenth General Council held in Frankfort on the Main, Germany, August 3–13, 1964, on the theme of the ancient prayer of the church, "Come, Creator Spirit!"

34. There have been several brother combinations in the theological enterprise. Two prominent families in the Reformed tradition of our century are the Niebuhrs (Richard and Rein-hold) and the Baillies (Donald and John).

35. Von Campenhausen, *The Fathers of the Greek Church,* p. 122.

36. The "Three Hierarchs" are particularly so honored by the Orthodox for their ecclesiological outlooks. These fathers in their theologizing conceived of an ecumenical church which would include the Old Testament narrative beginning with Adam and would eventually involve the total restoration of

mankind. See "The Ecclesiology of the Three Hierarchs," *The Greek Orthodox Theological Review*, Vol. VI, No. 2 (Winter, 1960–1961), pp. 135–185.

37. Von Campenhausen, *The Fathers of the Greek Church*, p. 140.

38. *Ibid.*, p. 157.

39. *Ibid.*, p. 158.

40. Florovsky, "Saint Gregory Palamas," *loc. cit.*, p. 169. From a positive standpoint, however, reference to the fathers was the usual method for the church to maintain continuity in its creedal and doctrinal statements.

41. *Ibid.*, pp. 175–176.

42. St. Basil the Great, *De Spiritu Sancto* XVIII.xliv.28, *The Nicene and Post-Nicene Fathers*, ed. by Philip Schaff (Christian Literature Co., 1895), Vol. VIII.

43. T. F. Torrance, "The Logic and Analogic of Biblical and Theological Statements in the Greek Fathers," *Theology in Reconstruction*, p. 31.

44. Ludwig Feuerbach in his classic book, *The Essence of Christianity* (Harper Torchbooks, The Cloister Library, Harper & Brothers, 1957), has pointed to an exaggerated but nevertheless severe criticism of this tendency in Western theologizing. See also in this regard the thesis of Leslie Dewart, *The Future of Belief: Theism in a World Come of Age.*

45. Torrance, *Theology in Reconstruction*, p. 31.

46. Georges Dejaifve, "East and West: Two Theologies, One Faith," *Rediscovering Eastern Christendom*, ed. by E. L. B. Fry and A. H. Armstrong, p. 51.

47. *Ibid.*

48. Vladimir Lossky, *The Mystical Theology of the Eastern Church*, p. 25.

49. *Ibid.*

50. John of Damascus, *Exposition of the Orthodox Faith* (*De Fide Orthodoxa*), I.iv.4, *The Nicene and Post-Nicene Fathers*, ed. by Philip Schaff and Henry Wace, Second Series (Charles Scribner's Sons, 1899), Vol. IX.

51. Compare the Orthodox attitude with what John Calvin writes in his *Institutes of the Christian Religion*, especially

Book I, "The Knowledge of God the Creator," in Chs. i and ii.
Is there not room for a creative synthesis of outlooks here?

52. Dejaifve, "East and West," in Fry and Armstrong (eds.),
Rediscovering Eastern Christendom, p. 52.

53. *Ibid.*

54. *Ibid.*

55. *Ibid.*, p. 54.

Chapter III.
MISSIONS, PROSELYTISM, AND THE FUTURE

1. Such were the thoughts of Protestant Samuel McCrea
Cavert regarding Orthodoxy at the initial stages of encounter.
Note his admission in *On the Road to Unity* (Harper & Broth-
ers, 1961), pp. 78–79.

2. A. Yannoulatos, " 'Porefthendes' an Inter-Orthodox Missionary Centre," *Porefthendes*, No. 11 (July-September, 1961),
p. 36.

3. See A. Yannoulatos, "Orthodoxy and Mission," an address
delivered at the General Assembly of Syndesmos (Finland,
July, 1964), *St. Vladimir's Seminary Quarterly*, Vol. 8, No. 3
(1964), pp. 139–148.

4. *Porefthendes*, No. 10 (April-June, 1961), p. 18.

5. *Ibid.*

6. According to Timothy Ware, "African Orthodoxy did not
arise through the preaching of [Orthodox] missionaries from
the traditional Orthodox lands, but was a spontaneous movement among Africans themselves. The founders of the Ugandan
Orthodox Church—both of them still very much alive—are two
native Ugandans, Rauben Sebanja Mukasa Spartas and Oba-
diah Kabanda Basajjakitalo. Originally brought up as Anglicans, they were converted to Orthodoxy in the 1920's, not
as a result of personal contact with other Orthodox, but through
their own reading and study" (*The Orthodox Church*, pp. 196–
197).

7. *Porefthendes*, No. 11 (July-September, 1961), p. 38.

8. To my knowledge there is no comprehensive book on the
history of Orthodox missions. The only recent books of impor-

tance are limited to Russian missions and written by Josef Glazik (see Bibliography). See also "Orthodoxy and Mission," *The International Review of Missions*, Vol. LIV, No. 215 (1965).

9. Cf. *Porefthendes*, No. 10 (April-June, 1961), pp. 28–30.

10. John Meyendorff, "Orthodox Missions in the Middle Ages," *History Lessons for Tomorrow's Mission*, ed. by the World's Student Christian Federation, p. 102.

11. *Ibid.*

12. *Ibid.*, p. 113.

13. An article, "Missionary Aims and the Russian Orthodox Church," by Archpriest Vsevolod Spiller, Prior of the Nikolo-Kuznetsky Church, Moscow, in *The International Review of Missions*, Vol. LII (1963), pp. 197 f., contends that mission "was much more closely related to the work of the church as a whole than was the case in the West."

14. Meyendorff, "Orthodox Missions in the Middle Ages," *loc. cit.*, pp. 106–107.

15. *Ibid.*, p. 108.

16. *Ibid.*

17. Of course, the defeat of the Tartar khan by the czar gave a psychological atmosphere which was helpful to Bishop Gurji's work, even though the czar made the stipulation "that the conversion of the native inhabitants was to be achieved by persuasion and gentleness and that every resort to violence should be systematically avoided" (*ibid.*, p. 109).

18. *Ibid.* For further description of Orthodox missionary activity among the Muslims, see *Birbeck and the Russian Church*, ed. by Athelstan Riley, especially Ch. XVI, "Russian Missions to the Mohammedans." It is my opinion that the potential for greater dialogue with Islam lies with the Orthodox. See Chapter IX, on icons, for the suggestion of the Islamic scholar Kenneth Cragg.

19. Meyendorff, "Orthodox Missions in the Middle Ages," *loc. cit.*, p. 110.

20. *Ibid.*, pp. 113–114

21. S. Bolshakoff, "Orthodox Missions Today," *The International Review of Missions*, July, 1953, p. 277.

22. Cf. Alexander Schmemann's chapter "The Missionary Imperative in the Orthodox Tradition," *The Theology of the Christian Mission*, ed. by Gerald H. Anderson (McGraw-Hill Book Company, Inc., 1961), pp. 250–257.

23. On the negative side, Ernst Benz comments that "national tensions are forever asserting themselves. Grave difficulties crop up in any collaboration among Greeks, Arabs and Slavs. And in Syria, Palestine and Egypt, joint work between the Greek and Arab or Coptic portions of the Church has been impeded by rivalries for spiritual and practical leadership within the Church" (*The Eastern Orthodox Church*, p. 212). Aware of this rivalry, Alexander A. Bogolepov in his book *Toward an American Orthodox Church* reveals the desire of many Orthodox in America to go beyond nationalistic backgrounds. The movement of Western Rite Orthodoxy is another expression to rediscover the universality of Orthodoxy beyond ethnic consciousness. See W. Jardine Grisbrooke, "The Eastern Rite in the Western Parish," *St. Vladimir's Seminary Quarterly*, Vol. 9, No. 2 (1965), pp. 75–82; and Wm. S. Schneirla, "The Western Rite in the Orthodox Church," *St. Vladimir's Seminary Quarterly*, Vol. 2, No. 2 (1958), pp. 20–44.

24. Historically, the Orthodox point to Protestant missionaries who desired to work beside them in the Middle East but who for numerous reasons founded Protestant churches which were made up largely of former Orthodox Christians, while the declared goal of evangelism among the Muslims remained relatively untouched. This is also true of the harsh attitude of some Greek Orthodox (even today) toward the Roman Catholic Church and the latter's maintenance of Uniate churches in communion with Rome.

25. Protestants (particularly Anglicans) and Roman Catholics point to the questionable converts in Uganda and Kenya as proselytism by the Orthodox mission rather than the actual carrying of the gospel to non-Christians. This situation remains a contested point of debate among the churches concerned.

26. Taken from the World Council of Churches' report on proselytism, *The Ecumenical Review*, Vol. IX, No. 1 (October, 1956), pp. 4–5.

Chapter IV.
EASTERN CATHOLICITY

1. An excellent discussion, although too brief, on catholicity is found in *The Ecumenical Review,* Vol. XVI, No. 1 (October, 1963), with articles by Lukas Vischer, Vitaly Borovoy, and Claude Welch. See also John Meyendorff, "The Orthodox Concept of the Church," *St. Vladimir's Seminary Quarterly,* Vol. 6, No. 2 (1962), pp. 59–71; and Hendrikus Berkhof, *De Katholiciteit der Kerk* (Nijkerk, The Netherlands, 1962), translated and condensed by S. K. Hanhart in the *Bulletin,* Vol. 6, No. 1, of the World Alliance of Reformed and Presbyterian Churches.

2. See *Faith and Order Trends,* Vol. 3, No. 2 (March, 1963).

3. Pope Paul VI sought to support this concern by his pilgrimage to the Holy Land and his encounter with Ecumenical Patriarch Athenagoras and the other Eastern bishops. The trip illustrated dramatically the pope's desire to associate catholicity beyond the Italian and Vatican borders. His later journeys to India and Turkey again highlighted the fact that catholicity implies more than the existing Latin emphasis in the Roman Church.

4. The Council of Lyon (1274) and the Council of Florence (1439) are two of the better known but ill-fated attempts of reunion initiated by the West.

5. For further discussion on *sobornost'*, see Sergius Bulgakov, *The Orthodox Church;* and V. Illyin, "The Nature and the Meaning of the Term 'Sobornost','" *Sobornost'*, March, 1935, pp. 5–7.

6. Alexis S. Khomiakov, *The Church Is One,* p. 14.

7. For more information on Orthodox Church organization, see John Meyendorff, "Ecclesiastical Organization in the History of Orthodoxy," *St. Vladimir's Seminary Quarterly,* Vol. IV, No. 1 (1960), pp. 2–23; and S. Troitzky "Autocephality in the Church," *One Church,* Vol. XVIII, Nos. 3–4 (1964), pp. 112–116.

8. As Orthodox theologian Boris Bobrinskoy rightly observes, "In the ecumenical consciousness, the catholicity of the Church is appearing more and more, not merely as a tradi-

tional notion of the historical churches, but as the common goal towards which all the churches are marching together —as the aim of the ecumenical movement itself" (p. 513, "The Continuity of the Church and Orthodoxy," *The Ecumenical Review,* October, 1964, pp. 512–529).

9. Serge Bolshakoff, *The Eastern Churches Quarterly,* Vol. X (1953–1954), p. 233.

10. John Meyendorff, "Vatican II: Definitions or Search for Unity?" *St. Vladimir's Seminary Quarterly,* Vol. 7, No. 4 (1964), pp. 164–168. See also "Primacy and Primacies in the Orthodox Church," *ibid.,* Vol. 4, Nos. 2–3 (1960).

11. Meyendorff, "Vatican II," *loc. cit.,* pp. 167–168.

12. *Ibid.*

13. N. A. Nissiotis, "Is the Vatican Council Really Ecumenical?" *The Ecumenical Review,* Vol. XVI, No. 4 (July, 1964), pp. 357–377; and his "Report on the Second Vatican Council," *ibid.,* Vol. XVIII, No. 2 (1966), pp. 190–206.

14. Nissiotis, "Is the Vatican Council Really Ecumenical?" *loc. cit.,* p. 358.

15. For the Orthodox, any official conversation with Roman Catholics must be on equal terms ecclesiastically.

16. Nissiotis, "Is the Vatican Council Really Ecumenical?" *loc. cit.,* p. 363.

17. Georges Dejaifve, " 'Sobornost' ' or Papacy," *The Eastern Churches Quarterly,* Parts I–IV, Vol. X, Nos. 1–4 (Spring-Winter, 1953), p. 119.

18. *Ibid.,* pp. 119–121.

19. C. Welch, "Catholicity," *The Ecumenical Review,* Vol. XVI, No. 1 (October, 1963), p. 38.

20. Visser 't Hooft, former Secretary of the World Council of Churches, has observed that today Orthodox and Protestants are speaking to each other as *equal partners* in dialogue ("Between Constantinople and Rome," *The Christian Century,* September 9, 1962, p. 1107). For further discussion, refer to Chapter I.

21. Cf. C. S. Calian, "Beyond East and West," *Dialog,* Vol. 7 (Summer, 1968), and also in *The Reformed and Presbyterian World,* June, 1968.

THE VISIBLE AND INVISIBLE CHURCH

1. Sometimes the distinction between the *ecclesia triumphans* in heaven and the *ecclesia militans* on earth is used to
stand for the invisible and visible church respectively. However, this practice can be misconstrued to indicate that the
invisible church is equated with the company of the redeemed
in heaven (*ecclesia triumphans*). While this may well be true,
it goes beyond the empirical reality of the church, with which
the basic concept of the visible and invisible church sought to
deal in a creative way. The visible/invisible distinction is addressing itself to the *ecclesia militans* on earth and is raising
the question whether the visible church is inclusive enough to
include all true believers or whether there are true Christians
not affiliated with any organizational visible church.

2. G. H. Joyce, "Church," *The Catholic Encyclopedia*, pp.
744–761. See also Hans Kung, *Structures of the Church*, especially pages 30–70; G. Thils, "Marks of the Church," *New
Catholic Encyclopedia*, prepared by an editorial staff at the
Catholic University of America (McGraw-Hill Book Company, Inc., 1967), Vol. 8, pp. 240–241; and Vatican II's *Dogmatic Constitution on the Church (De Ecclesia)*.

3. Thils, "Marks of the Church," *loc. cit.*, p. 241.

4. Joyce, "Church," *loc. cit.*, p. 752.

5. Cyprian, "The Unity of the Catholic Church," *Early Latin
Theology: Selections from Tertullian, Cyprian, Ambrose, and
Jerome*, tr. and ed. by S. L. Greenslade (The Library of Chris-
tian Classics, Vol. V: The Westminster Press, 1956), pp. 127–

6. Augustine, *City of God, passim; On Baptism* III.xix.26
(Migne, *Patrologiae cursus completus, series Latina* 43. 152;
tr. *The Nicene and Post-Nicene Fathers*, Vol. IV, p. 445). Also,
there is Augustine's saying in reference to the church, "Many
sheep are without, and many wolves are within" (*John's Gospel* XLV. 12 [*MPL* 35. 1725; tr. *NPNF*, VII. 253 f.]).

7. Luther was the first to apply the visible/invisible concept
to the Protestant context. He actually favored the word "hidden" (*abscondita*) to *invisibilis*. (Cf. *Ad librum Ex Mag.*

Nostri Mag. Ambrosii Catharni . . . Responsio, 1521, ed. Weimar Ausgabe, VII, p. 722).

8. Calvin, *Institutes of the Christian Religion,* IV.i.4 (The Library of Christian Classics, Vol. XXI, p. 1016).

9. Geddes MacGregor, *Corpus Christi,* p. 74.

10. Jaroslav Pelikan in his book *The Riddle of Roman Catholicism* has rightly appraised this period of history in terms of "The Tragic Necessity of the Reformation" (p. 45)—tragic, because it consisted in the loss on both sides of some of the very things each claimed to be of the essence to the church in its defense against the other.

11. The Reformed tradition is mindful of the fact that the church is a human institution and is subject to error even though it is also a divinely instituted *congregatio* gathered to wait upon its Lord. Therefore, it can only be considered a "type" of the incarnation, which is recognized in the maxim of the Reformed tradition, *Ecclesia Reformata, semper reformanda.*

12. Wilhelm Niesel, *The Theology of Calvin,* p. 18.

13. This conclusion is, of course, contrary to the way Roman Catholic theologians traditionally view the Protestant understanding of the church. Cf. Moehler's comments on refutations of Luther's and Calvin's teachings on the church (*Symbolism,* pp. 402–416).

14. This is not to say that there is complete absence of any criterion to indicate a faithful church. The Reformers set up standards in terms of the preaching of the word, the administration of the sacraments, and the discipline of the members who make up the household of faith. The point that is emphasized above is that there remains the problem of human weakness. The total visibility of the church is beyond our measurable horizon; it can only be seen in God's unmeasurable horizon.

15. "The 'Johannine' character of Orthodoxy is supposed to contrast with the 'Petrinism' and 'Paulinism' of other Christian confessions. Such an idea seems to have originated in the romantic, religious atmosphere which surrounded both the Russian Slavophils and German exegesis and philosophy round about the forties of the last century. It has left lasting traces,

recognizable, for instance, in the *Peter and John* of Father Sergius Bulgakov and in the *Three Dialogues* of Vladimir Soloviev (where Pope Peter II represents the Roman Church, Professor Pauli, Protestantism, and the saintly elder John, Orthodoxy)," (*Orthodox Spirituality: An Outline of the Orthodox Ascetical and Mystical Tradition,* a monk of the Eastern Church [published for the Fellowship of SS. Alban and Sergius; London: S.P.C.K., 1945], pp. 3–4.)

16. Lossky, *The Mystical Theology of the Eastern Church,* p. 9.

17. Bulgakov, *The Orthodox Church,* p. 14.

18. There is no question that there is a danger of speaking in terms of visible/invisible church and thereby escaping our responsibility for having visible unity of the divided church, thinking that such unity can be found only in an invisible church. As Barth aptly puts it, "Where the Church is divided in the way which now concerns us, the division reaches right down to its invisible being, its relationship to God and Jesus Christ and the Holy Spirit, and it develops from this, the external division being the result of an internal disruption, so that neither individuals nor the whole Church can overcome it by a flight to the invisible, but only by a healing of both its visible and its invisible hurt" (*Church Dogmatics,* IV/1, p. 678; *Die Kirchliche Dogmatik,* IV/1, s. 757).

19. Cf. K. L. Schmidt, "The Church" in Gerhard Kittel (ed.), *Theologisches Wörterbuch zum Neuen Testament,* Vol. 3, pp. 537–539, found in *Bible Key Words,* tr. and ed. by J. R. Coates (Harper & Brothers, 1951), pp. 66–69.

20. It should be cited that Luther himself equated the *ecclesia invisibilis* with the *ecclesia (spiritualis) sola fide perceptibilis* (see Weimar Ausgabe, VII, 710—the oldest passage).

21. Barth, *Church Dogmatics,* IV/1, p. 685; *Kirchliche Dogmatik,* IV/1, s. 757.

22. Bishop Lesslie Newbigin, *The Household of God* (Friendship Press, 1954), p. 114.

23. Roman Catholic theologian Yves Congar seems also to prefer the concept of the mystical body of Christ (*Divided Christendom: A Catholic Study of the Problem of Reunion,*

tr. by M. A. Bousfield [Geoffrey Bles, Ltd., 1939], pp. 222–226).

24. Note that Augustin Cardinal Bea has in part the same intent as the above statement when he replies: "Some theologians say: Christ has reserved this perfect unity—visible and invisible—of all Christians in one Church, until the Church reaches her final glory at the end of time. There is no objection to this, if we mean that the Church on earth is on the *way* to this perfect unity, that the unity which Christ has already given to the Church is in the process of perfection" (*The Unity of Christians*, p. 185).

Chapter VI.
THE HIERARCHY AND THE LAITY

1. *Presbyterian Life,* November 15, 1965, p. 33.

2. *The Layman in Christian History,* ed. by Stephen C. Neill and Hans-Ruedi Weber, p. 298. See C. S. Calian, "The Man in the Pew," *The Catholic World,* December, 1966.

3. "If in the Bible the word 'lay' is rare and somewhat vague, it contains, however, a very rich and clear notion of the *laos,* the people of God. At the side of a functional priesthood (the levitical, priestly caste), Scripture speaks of the universal priesthood of the People of God in its totality." (Paul Evdokimov, *The Struggle with God,* p. 195.)

4. *Ibid.,* p. 196.

5. *Ibid.*

6. *Ibid.*

7. Alexander Schmemann's helpful booklet, *Clergy and Laity in the Orthodox Church* (St. Vladimir's Seminary Press) is somewhat overzealous in attributing "clericalism" (p. 8) primarily to Roman Catholics and Protestants. It is understandable that Schmemann is seeking here to give an identifying characteristic of Orthodoxy to Orthodox readers living in predominately non-Orthodox environments.

8. *Ibid.*

9. Evdokimov, *The Struggle with God,* p. 201. Along with the sacrament of Chrism, there is the act of consecration through the rite of tonsure. This rite highlights the totalitarian

and absolute character of the lay priestliness, for the rite "is identical with that performed for one entering a monastic order. The prayer asks: 'Bless thy servant who has come to offer thee as first gifts the tonsure of the hair of his head.' Its symbolic meaning is unmistakable—it is the total offering of his life" (*ibid.*, pp. 201–202).

10. According to Professor Evdokimov, "This perfect equality of nature in all the members of the Church corresponds to the fundamentally homogeneous character of Orthodox spirituality. Likewise there exists no separation into the teaching Church and the Church taught, but it is the total Church that teaches the Church, just as it is in the whole of its teaching that the Gospel is addressed to each and all" (*ibid.*, p. 200).

11. Neill and Weber, *The Layman in Christian History,* p. 281.

12. The sacrament of Holy Chrism for the Orthodox is essentially the sacrament of strength in order to be the guardians of the faith.

13. Evdokimov, *The Struggle with God,* p. 197. In the New Testament generally, the term *presbyteros* ("elder") is used to designate this clerical ministry, whereas the term *hieros* applies to the priesthood of the laity. See such passages as Rev. 20:6; 1:6; 5:10 and I Peter 2:5.

14. *Ibid.*

15. Nicolas Zernov, *Orthodox Encounter,* p. 84. For a glimpse of the life of a traditional Orthodox priest, see Nicolai Lyeskov, *The Cathedral Folk* (Alfred A. Knopf, Inc., 1934).

16. Zernov, *Orthodox Encounter,* p. 84. This communal understanding of the church is rooted in patristic thought. The word *ecclesia* for Ignatius implies a local community, the people themselves, gathered together for worship and communion. "Take heed, then, often to come together to give thanks to God and show forth His praise. For when you assemble frequently in the same place (*epi to auto*), the powers of Satan are destroyed, and the destruction at which he aims is prevented by the unity of your faith." (Ignatius, *Eph.* 13, quoted in John S. Romanides, "The Ecclesiology of St. Ignatius of Antioch," *Greek Theological Review,* Vol. 7 [1962], p. 63.)

17. See Hans Kung, *Structures of the Church;* Bishop Athena-

goras, "Priesthood as a Sacrament," *The Greek Orthodox Theological Review*, Vol. 3 (1957), pp. 168–181; and Johannes Panagopolous, "An Orthodox Study of Ministerial Office," *Journal of Ecumenical Studies*, Vol. 4 (1967), pp. 27–46.

18. N. Afanassieff, "The Ministry of the Laity in the Church," *The Ecumenical Review*, Vol. X (1958), p. 258.

19. *Ibid.*, p. 259.

20. Schmemann, *Clergy and Laity in the Orthodox Church*, p. 13.

21. *Ibid.*, p. 15. Cyril Eastwood (*The Royal Priesthood of the Faithful*, pp. 239–240) from a Protestant viewpoint refers to the *oneness* of the body in the following terms: initiation to priesthood (baptism), realized priesthood (confirmation), and representative priesthood (clerical orders).

22. Max Thurian, *Consecration of the Layman*, p. 100. See also Vatican II's "Decree on the Apostolate of the Laity"; Lukas Vischer, *Ye Are Baptized* (Department on the Laity, World Council of Churches, 1964), and Elizabeth E. McCort, "Changes in Theory and Practice of Confirmation in the (United) Presbyterian Church in the United States of America, 1789–1958" (unpublished dissertation, Union Theological Seminary, 1967).

23. See B. Reicke, "The Constitution of the Primitive Church in the Light of Jewish Documents," *The Scrolls and the New Testament*, ed. by Krister Stendahl (Harper & Brothers, 1957). Reicke finds both in Acts and in the Qumran Manual monarchic, oligarchic, and democratic tendencies coexisting in organic unity among these early Christian and Jewish communities. Cf. Kung, *Structures of the Church*, especially Ch. VII.

24. Afanassieff, "The Ministry of the Laity in the Church," *loc. cit.*, pp. 258–259.

25. Elie Melia, "An Orthodox Point of View on the Problem of Authority in the Church," *Problems of Authority*, ed. by John M. Todd, p. 107.

26. Romanides, "The Ecclesiology of St. Ignatius of Antioch," *loc. cit.*, p. 67.

27. *Ibid.*, p. 67.

28. *Ibid.*, p. 68.

29. *Ibid.*, p. 71.

30. George Khodr, "The Diaconate in the Orthodox Church," *"The Ministry of Deacons* (Geneva: World Council of Churches, 1965), p. 43. The anachronistic state of the diaconate was due in part to the incorporating and institutionalizing of the laity in the nineteenth century in the Eastern Patriarchates.

31. The World Council of Churches has carried on a lively dialogue regarding the diaconate in the monograph *The Ministry of Deacons* from many points of view and also in other studies entitled *The Role of the "Diakonia" of the Church in Contemporary Society* (1966) and *The Deaconess* (1966). See also *The Documents of Vatican II,* especially with reference to the diaconate.

Chapter VII.
CHURCH, STATE, AND SOCIAL CONSCIOUSNESS

1. Oscar Cullmann, *The State in the New Testament,* p. 91.

2. Deno John Geanakoplos, *Byzantine East and Latin West,* pp. 60–61. Professor Geanakoplos contends that the term "caesaropapism" applied to Byzantine political theory as initially developed by Eusebius is not satisfactory. The term implies an all-pervasive imperial control over both temporal and spiritual affairs and fails to express the actual symphonic duet as experienced in practice. While I concur with Geanakoplos that a more satisfactory term needs to be found, there remains the general observation that a propensity toward caesaropapism exists throughout much of Byzantine history.

3. Gregory T. Armstrong, "Church and State Relations: The Changes Wrought by Constantine," *The Journal of Bible and Religion,* Vol. XXXII, No. 1, pp. 6–7.

4. The consultation was held at Aarhus, Denmark, August 11–15, 1964.

5. In Rome's pre-Christian days, civil officials served as priests during the period of sacrifices, and no priestly caste as such existed (Geanakoplos, *Byzantine East and Latin West,* p. 60).

6. Sherrard, *The Greek East and the Latin West,* p. 92.

7. Deno John Geanakoplos, "Church Building and 'Caesaropapism,'" *Greek-Roman and Byzantine Studies,* Vol. 7, No. 2

(1966), pp. 167–186. Note that during the reign of Justinian, ninety-six churches were built, fifty-five of these explicitly with imperial funds for the use of converted "Hellenes" (*ibid.*, p. 183). See also, G. T. Armstrong, "Imperial Church Building and Church-State Relations, A.D. 313–363," *Church History,* March, 1967, pp. 3–17.

8. Geanakoplos, "Church Building and 'Caesaropapism,' *loc. cit.,* p. 186.

9. S. L. Greenslade, *Church and State from Constantine to Theodosius,* pp. 21–22, quoting Constantine in N. H. Baynes, *Constantine and the Christian Church* (Proceedings of the British Academy, Vol. XV, 1929).

10. "*Quid imperatori cum ecclesia?,*" *ibid.,* p. 43.

11. When Julian ascended the throne, he literally attempted to turn the clock back to the Empire's former pagan days by establishing a new ideology of Hellenism. (Armstrong, "Imperial Church Building and Church-State Relations, A.D. 313–363," *loc. cit.,* p. 16.)

12. In Byzantine church-state relations, the power balance has often been determined in direct ratio to the strength of the personalities who confronted each other at various times throughout its history.

13. See Christopher B. Coleman, *Constantine the Great and Christianity,* especially Part III and the Appendix.

14. Cf. Matthew Spinka, "Patriarch Nikon and the Subjection of the Russian Church to the State," *Church History,* Vol. 10 (1946), pp. 347–366.

15. For an eyewitness account on Soviet Armenia, see C. S. Calian, "Encounter with a Communist Republic," *Presbyterian Life,* April 15, 1966. The time is now ripe for a creative exchange of ideas between Communists and Christians. In fact, the dialogue has already begun as dramatized in Roger Garaudy's book, *From Anathema to Dialogue: A Marxist Challenge to the Christian Churches,* tr. by Luke O'Neill (Herder & Herder, Inc., 1966). See also in this connection, C. S. Calian, "Dialogue in an Age of Convergence," *The Christian Century,* May 24, 1967, pp. 681–683.

16. V. I. Lenin, *On Religion* (Moscow: Progress Publishers, 1965), p. 8.

17. See Edward Wakin, "Egypt's Christian Minority," *The Christian Century*, March 11, 1964, pp. 332–334; and Otto F. A. Meinardus, *The Attitudes of the Orthodox Copts Towards the Islamic State from the 7th to the 12th Century*, Ostkirchliche Studien, 13. Band, Heft 2/3, pp. 153–170.

18. Ware, *Eustratios Argenti*, pp. 3–4.

19. See *Time*, September 9, 1966, pp. 84–86. Cf. John S. Romanides, "The Orthodox Churches on Church-State Relations and Religious Liberty," *A Journal of Church and State*, Vol. IV, No. 2 (1964), pp. 178–189 (this particular issue is devoted to the theme of religious liberty).

20. Cf. Adolf von Harnack, *What Is Christianity?* (G. P. Putnam Sons, 1901), p. 217.

21. This rendering of the prayer is in contemporary prose. A more literal English translation can be found in *The Orthodox Liturgy*, Liturgy of St. John Chrysostom and St. Basil the Great, ed. by the Fellowship of SS. Alban and Sergius (London: S.P.C.K., 1960), pp. 78–79. For the original Greek, see F. E. Brightman, *Liturgies: Eastern and Western*, Vol. I.

22. Father Georges Florovsky summarizes the role of monasticism in saying that it "was an attempt to *fulfil* the Christian obligation, to organize human life exclusively on a Christian basis, in opposition to 'the world.' . . . Monasticism attracts now not only as a school of contemplation, but also as a school of obedience, as a social experiment, as an experiment in common life. Here lies the modern thrill of the cloister" ("Empire and Desert: Antinomies of Christian History," *Greek Theological Review*, Vol. III, No. 2 [1957], pp. 157–158). See also Chapter XI, on "Spirituality, Monasticism, and Relevance." For a more expanded treatment of the social importance of eschatology in Orthodox thought, see C. S. Calian, *The Significance of Eschatology in the Thoughts of Nicolas Berdyaev* or *Berdyaev's Philosophy of Hope* (title of revised edition).

23. Cf. Sergius Bulgakoff, *Social Teaching in Modern Russian Orthodox Theology* (Seabury-Western Theological Seminary, 1934).

24. Demetrios J. Constantelos, *The Greek Orthodox Church*, pp. 58–59. For a more extensive treatment of *philanthrōpia* in

Byzantine history, see by the same author, *Byzantine Philanthropy and Social Welfare.*

Chapter VIII.
EASTER AND THE EUCHARISTIC WORSHIP

1. Paul Verghese, "Relation Between Baptism, Confirmation, and the Eucharist in the Syrian Orthodox Church," *Studia Liturgica*, Vol. IV, No. 2, p. 81.

2. Georges Florovsky, "Orthodox," *Ways of Worship*, ed. by Pehr Edwall *et al.*, p. 53.

3. Alexander Schmemann, *Introduction to Liturgical Theology*, p. 24.

4. Armand J. Jacopin, "The Eastern Liturgy in the American Context," *Diakonia*, Vol. 2, No. 1 (1967), p. 19.

5. Lukas Vischer, "Joint Celebration of the Resurrection of Christ," *World Council of Churches, Division of Studies, Commission on Faith and Order*, June, 1965, p. 1. This is an excellent summarization of the question of Easter dates with an appendix of documents discussing the issue by both secular and church authorities.

6. Paul Evdokimov, "Nature," *Scottish Journal of Theology*, Vol. 18, No. 1 (1965), p. 15.

7. Alexander Schmemann, *Sacraments and Orthodoxy*, p. 16. It is interesting to note that there exists a similarity of spirit between Quakers (traditional type) and Orthodox. While there is a marked outward contrast in their respective worship experiences, their inward attitude is similar, for both consider all of life to be sacramental.

8. *Ibid.*

9. *Ibid.*, pp. 19–20.

10. See Chapter X for a discussion of the Epiclesis.

11. Schmemann, *Sacraments and Orthodoxy*, p. 42.

12. Florovsky, "Orthodox," in Edwall *et al.* (eds.), *Ways of Worship*, pp. 59–60.

13. "The word 'community' is still somewhat of a stranger to our postindividualist modern world. . . . Worship has to be in community. He who has not felt in his bones his own solidarity

with the rest of mankind has not yet known the heart of worship." (Paul Verghese, *The Joy of Freedom: Eastern Worship
and Modern Man,* p. 19.)

14. The word "sacrament" implies in Western theology a
sign and seal of a specific grace. The East is not used to thinking in such terms; it prefers to speak of a *mystērion.* The Eucharistic liturgy shows forth through a mystery the passion, death,
and resurrection of Christ. "The 'showing forth' or the celebration is the mystery, not the 'elements,' though the elements are
an integral part of the mystery." (Verghese, "Relation Between
Baptism, 'Confirmation,' and the Eucharist," *loc. cit.,* p. 82.)

15. *Ibid.,* p. 84.

16. T. Ware, "Intercommunion: The Decisions of Vatican II
and the Orthodox Standpoint," *Sobornost',* Series 5, No. 4
(1966), p. 260.

17. "Cardinal Lercaro on *Communicatio in Sacris* with the
Orthodox," *One in Christ,* Vol. I, No. 2 (1965), p. 188.

18. Professor Evdokimov argues that intercommunion demands previous dogmatic agreement on the elements of faith.
"Now the dogmatic points, properly so called, which separate
us [Catholics and Orthodox] at the present time—the *filioque*
and the Immaculate Conception—do not present insurmount-
able obstacles. The Papal Primacy [he adds] is a matter of
Canon Law, not a dogmatic issue." (Ware, "Intercommunion,"
loc. cit., p. 270.) See also Henry Hill, "Father Sergius Bulgakov
and Intercommunion," *Sobornost',* Winter, 1966, pp. 272–276.

19. N. A. Nissiotis, "Worship, Eucharist, and 'Intercommunion': An Orthodox Reflection," *Studia Liturgica,* September,
1963, p. 219.

20. Father P. Verghese claims that there exists "in the Western Reformed and Lutheran traditions a definitely anti-liturgi-
cal bias which now finds expression in the attitudes of the
neo-Bonhoefferians and neo-Bultmannians and the decreasing
tribe of Barthians and Brunnerites" (*The Joy of Freedom,*
p. 12).

21. See Rev. D. J. Constantelos' comparative and statistical
study on "The Holy Scriptures in Greek Orthodox Worship,"
The Greek Orthodox Theological Review, Vol. XII, No. 1
(1966), pp. 7–83. See also Georges Florovsky, "Scripture and

Tradition: An Orthodox Point of View," *Dialog*, Vol. 2 (1965), pp. 288–293.

22. Verghese, *The Joy of Freedom*, p. 24.

23. For a listing of the various vernacular languages in the Eastern liturgies, see Verghese, *The Joy of Freedom*, pp. 42–43. Orthodox churches generally encourage the use of the vernacular. Fr. S. Salaville regards this as one important factor contrasting Orthodox and Roman Catholics. However, the problem for the East is that the vernacular is often in its ancient forms (e.g., Old Slavonic or classical Armenian) rather than in the more contemporary idiom of the people. In practice it is almost equivalent to a foreign language.

24. *The Orthodox Liturgy*, p. 75.

Chapter IX.
The Art and Mission of the Icon

1. Philip Sherrard, "The Art of the Icon," *Sobornost'*, Series 4, No. 6 (1962), p. 295.

2. Paul Evdokimov, "The Meaning of Icons," *One in Christ*, Vol. III, No. 2 (1967), p. 171. See also by the same author, *L'Orthodoxie*, especially pp. 216–238; and Sergius Bulgakov, "Religion and Art," *The Church of God*, ed. by E. L. Mascall.

3. Evdokimov, "The Meaning of Icons," *loc. cit.*

4. *Ibid.*, p. 172.

5. Sherrard, "The Art of the Icon," *loc. cit.*, p. 295.

6. *Ibid.*, p. 297.

7. *Ibid.*

8. *Ibid.*, p. 297–298.

9. *Ibid.*

10. Leonide Ouspensky, "The Problem of the Iconostasis," *St. Vladimir's Seminary Quarterly*, Vol. 8, No. 4 (1964), p. 193. From a historical viewpoint, a curtain rather than a screen was used as an *iconostasis*. The Armenian and Abyssinian churches, which are non-Byzantine, still use curtains today in place of the *iconostasis*. According to Ouspensky, with the emergence of an Orthodoxy of the Western rite, churches without *iconostases* have begun to appear, especially here in the Western hemisphere (*ibid.*, p. 186).

11. Benz, *The Eastern Orthodox Church*, p. 9.

12. Ware, *The Orthodox Church*, p. 262. For the Orthodox, Mariology is an extension of Christology and the two aspects must always be seen in an organic relationship to each other. As Christ is the New Adam, Mary is the New Eve, whose life exemplified the monastic ideal of obedience and love. See in connection with Mary, Heiko A. Oberman, "The Virgin Mary in Evangelical Perspective," *Journal of Ecumenical Studies*, Vol. I, No. 2 (1964), pp. 271–298.

13. See Christos Giannaras, "An Orthodox Comment on 'the Death of God,'" *Sobornost'*, Series 5, No. 4 (1966), pp. 249–257.

14. Ware, *The Orthodox Church*, p. 39. See also the Definition of the Second Council of Nicaea (the seventh Ecumenical Council, 787, *Documents of the Christian Church*, ed. by Henry S. Bettenson (Oxford University Press, 1944), pp. 129–130. It has been speculated that the Islamic caliph Yazid II (in 721) in his iconoclastic edict influenced Leo III in his attack upon icons. Cf. A. A. Vasiliev, "The Iconoclastic Edict of the Caliph Yazid II A.D. 721," *Dumbarton Oaks Papers*, Vols. 9 and 10 (Harvard University Press, 1956), pp. 25–47.

15. Ware, *The Orthodox Church*, p. 42. See John of Damascus, "Concerning Images," *Exposition of the Orthodox Faith* (*De Fide Orthodoxa*), IV.xvi.88, *The Nicene and Post-Nicene Fathers*, Second Series, Vol. IX.

16. Leonide Ouspensky and Vladimir Lossky, *The Meaning of Icons*, p. 33.

17. *Ibid.*, p. 34.

18. Evdokimov, "The Meaning of Icons," *loc. cit.*, pp. 179–180.

19. Sherrard, "The Art of the Icon," *loc. cit.*, p. 304.

20. Karl Barth, *The Humanity of God*, p. 55. Cf. Finley Eversole, "Art and Sacrament," *The Christian Century*, Vol. LXXXI, No. 13 (1964), pp. 393–396. See also Wilhelm Niesel's objection to icons in his book, *The Gospel and the Churches*, pp. 158–160.

21. Evdokimov, "Nature," *loc. cit.*, pp. 18–19.

22. *Ibid.*

23. Ouspensky and Lossky, *The Meaning of Icons,* p. 55. See also Demetrios Dukan, "The Technique of Byzantine Icon-Painting," *Greek Theological Review,* Vol. 2 (1956), pp. 91–97, and John Papijohn, "Philosophical and Metaphysical Basis of Icon Veneration in the Eastern Orthodox Church," pp. 83–89.

24. John Meyendorff in his study of Byzantine-Islamic relations points out that through the centuries Byzantine Christianity has been kept on the defensive. ("Byzantine Views of Islam," pp. 131–132, *Dumbarton Oaks Papers,* Number Eighteen [J. J. Augustin, New York, 1964], pp. 115–132.)

25. Kenneth Cragg, "Idolatry and the Arts: An Islamic Dilemma," *Operation Reach,* March-April, 1961, p. 13 (St. Augustine's College, Canterbury, Kent, England). See also Norman Daniel, "Some Recent Developments in the Attitude of Christians Towards Islam," in Fry and Armstrong (eds.), *Rediscovering Eastern Christendom,* pp. 154–166 (including Bibliography).

26. Cragg, "Idolatry and the Arts," *loc. cit.,* p. 15. It is interesting to note that from a historic stance Byzantium played a part in bringing about new Islamic art forms. There are even cases of Byzantine artists decorating parts of the great Islamic mosques. Islamic art used Byzantine art when it needed iconographic expressions. Byzantine art thus became an essential ingredient in the formation of Islamic art—actually, it was not Byzantine *art* but the *themes* of Byzantine art that were used by Muslims (Oleg Grabar, "Islamic Art and Byzantium," *Dumbarton Oaks Papers,* Number Eighteen [J. J. Augustin, New York, 1964], p. 87).

27. Cragg, "Idolatry and the Arts," *loc. cit.,* p. 15.

28. *Ibid.,* p. 16.

Chapter X.
THE HOLY SPIRIT IN EAST AND WEST

1. Lossky, *The Mystical Theology of the Eastern Church,* p. 246.

2. *Ibid.,* p. 56. Lossky reports, "The *filioque* was the primor-

dial cause, the only dogmatic cause, of the breach between East and West."

3. According to Prof. S. L. Greenslade, of Oxford, the Filioque was part of a larger political issue of dominance between Patriarch Michael Cerularius and Pope Leo IX in 1054. Greenslade's point is that "the Patriarch of Constantinople made sure, probably quite deliberately, that there should be no *rapprochement* between himself and the Pope by requiring the Latins in Constantinople to conform to Greek usages and by extending this demand to the whole Latin church as a condition of communion" (*Schism in the Early Church*, p. 103). The political issue behind the Patriarch's insistence for conformity was his concern to maintain his autonomy.

4. Ware, *The Orthodox Church*, pp. 218–219.

5. George Every, *Misunderstandings Between East and West*, p. 119.

6. Gregory Nazianzus, *The Fifth Theological Oration*, XIV, p. 322, *Select Library of Nicene and Post-Nicene Fathers*, Vol. VII (Wm. B. Eerdmans Publishing Company, 1955).

7. *Ibid.*, Vol. IX; John of Damascus, *Exposition of the Orthodox Faith*, I.viii.10.

8. J. N. D. Kelly, *Early Christian Doctrines*, p. 263.

9. Ware, *The Orthodox Church*, p. 219.

10. T. F. Torrance notes the tendency toward the depersonalization of the Spirit by the West. An ecumenical theology must maintain the *homoousion* of the Spirit as well as of the Son. Torrance approaches the Orthodox position: "Perhaps it does not matter very much today whether the formal statement that the Spirit proceeds from the Son as well as from the Father is adopted or not (i.e., the *filioque*), but what does matter is whether Ecumenical Theology is fully prepared to maintain the *homoousion* both of the Son and of the Spirit for they belong inseparately together" (*Theology in Reconstruction*, p. 238).

11. "Latin Scholastic theology, emphasizing as it does the essence at the expense of the persons, comes near to turning God into an abstract idea. He becomes a remote and impersonal being, whose existence has to be proved by metaphysical

arguments—a God of the philosophers, not the God of Abraham, Isaac, and Jacob. Orthodoxy, on the other hand, has been far less concerned than the Latin West to find philosophical proofs of existence: what is important is not that a man should argue about the deity, but that he should have a direct and living encounter with a concrete and personal God." (Ware, *The Orthodox Church*, p. 222.)

12. Lossky, *The Mystical Theology of the Eastern Church*, p. 58.

13. Ware, *The Orthodox Church*, p. 222. Cf. Torrance, *Theology in Reconstruction*, pp. 209–228, "Spiritus Creator: A consideration of the teaching of St. Athanasius and St. Basil."

14. Perhaps from the Orthodox perspective it is not too much to say that the nineteenth General Council of the World Alliance of Reformed and Presbyterian Churches in Frankfort 1964, with its theme "Come, Creator Spirit!" is a manifestation of this need to give more attention to the person and work of the Holy Spirit. It is interesting to note here that the United Presbyterian Church's new *Book of Common Worship: Provisional Services* (and Lectionary for the Christian Year) omits the Filioque clause in the Nicene Creed in its Service for the Lord's Day (p. 25). Whether this was consciously done by the committee for the sake of unity between the East and West is not documented in the text. In any case, it is significant that the clause has been removed.

15. N. A. Nissiotis ("What Is Revealed by the Revelation in Christ?" *Theology and Life*, Vol. 6 [1963], pp. 37–48) regards as a bad sign in current theology the absence of a strong theology of the Holy Spirit along with a healthy Christology.

16. Ware, *The Orthodox Church*, pp. 219–220.

17. Lossky, *The Mystical Theology of the Eastern Church*, p. 62.

18. George S. Hendry, *The Holy Spirit in Christian Theology* (The Westminster Press, 1956), p. 52. Hendry also finds Barth's defense of the Filioque wanting, with Barth assigning the Spirit's role to the Son (*ibid.*, pp. 44–52). Hendry comments that the Roman Catholic Church's position on the Filioque "stands only as a monument to the constitutional

inability of the papacy to admit its mistake" ("From the Father and the Son: The Filioque After Nine Hundred Years," *Theology Today*, Vol. 11 [January, 1955], p. 453).

19. Irenaeus, *Against Heresies*, III. xxiv. 1, *The Ante-Nicene Fathers* (Wm. B. Eerdmans Publishing Company, 1950), Vol. I, p. 458.

20. Ware, *The Orthodox Church*, pp. 246–247. Prof. Joseph Haroutunian, of Chicago, parallels the Orthodox concern regarding the organic relationship of the Spirit to the church in expressing his own dismay at previous Protestant understanding of this relationship ("Come, Creator Spirit!" *Theology and Life*, Fall, 1963, pp. 209–210). See also George S. Hendry, "The Holy Spirit and the Renewal of the Church," *The Bulletin*, Moravian Theological Seminary, Fall, 1962, pp. 1–31.

21. A monk of the Eastern Church, *Orthodox Spirituality*, p. 77.

22. Ware, *The Orthodox Church*, p. 289.

23. *Ibid.*, pp. 289–290. It should be pointed out that the Orthodox "do not teach that consecration is effected solely by the *Epiclesis*, nor do they regard the Words of Institution as incidental and unimportant. On the contrary, they look upon the entire Eucharistic Prayer as forming a single and indivisible whole, so that the three main sections of the prayer—Thanksgiving, *Anamnesis, Epiclesis*—all form an integral part of the one act of consecration. But this of course means that if we are to single out a 'moment of consecration,' such a moment cannot come until the *Amen* of the *Epiclesis*" (*ibid.*).

24. Prof. J. J. von Allmen, of the University of Neuchâtel, in his article "Worship and the Holy Spirit" (*Studia Liturgica*, June, 1963, pp. 124–125), approached the Orthodox understanding of the role of the Holy Spirit in worship when he wrote: "The Holy Spirit induces worship because it transplants people into the eschatological world, because it makes the world to come present here and now, because it is the firstfruits of that world to come (II Cor. 1:22; 5:5; cf. Matt. 8:28; Acts 2:17; Rom. 8:23)."

25. John Meyendorff, *The Orthodox Church*, p. 73.

26. The term "sanctification" is more familiar to us in the West and can be considered similar to the meaning of *theosis*.

The term "justification," on the other hand, is actually foreign to the theological vocabulary of the Orthodox Christian. Justification implies a legal and rational meaning for the Latin West, and is contrary to the ways of thought in the Greek East. The Easterner is primarily concerned with sanctification and the Westerner is primarily concerned with justification; and yet the ultimate outcome of either position theologically is *reconciliation* between God and man in Jesus Christ. See Chapters IX and XI for further discussions on *theosis*.

27. Nissiotis, "What Is Revealed by the Revelation in Christ?" *loc. cit.*, p. 46. See also by the same author, "Interpreting Orthodoxy," *The Ecumenical Review,* October, 1961, pp. 4–28.

28. It is this need to get back to our true humanity that finds agreement among Protestant theologians such as Joseph Haroutunian, *God with Us,* Ch. 2, "The Spirit of the Living God"; and Paul Lehmann, *Ethics in a Christian Context,* especially Chs. III and IV. The Orthodox concept of *theosis* is a valuable theological aid at this point.

Chapter XI.
SPIRITUALITY, MONASTICISM, AND RELEVANCE

1. The substance of the discussions at this consultation of which I was a participant can be found in *The Ecumenical Review,* Vol. XV, No. 3 (1963).

2. N. A. Nissiotis, "Eastern and Western Theologians Study Together Spirituality," *ibid.,* p. 247.

3. *Ibid.,* p. 250.

4. John C. Bennett (ed.), *Christian Social Ethics in a Changing World,* pp. 83–84. Cf. Leslie Dewart, *The Future of Belief: Theism in a World Come of Age,* especially p. 188. For the quote on Athanasius, see his "On the Incarnation of the Word" (*De Incarnatione Verbi Dei*), 54, *The Nicene and Post-Nicene Fathers,* ed. by P. Schaff and H. Wace, Second Series, Vol. IV (Wm. B. Eerdmans Publishing Company, 1953), p. 65.

5. Hesychasm has a long and involved history. It refers specifically to the spiritual practices articulated on Mt. Athos

and brought to prominence in the fourteenth century under
the leadership of Gregory Palamas. The word "hesychasm"
signifies quietude and spiritual vigilance through which process the believer has the possibility of witnessing the Divine
Light, which is the highest fulfillment (*theosis*) for the individual.

6. Nicolas Berdyaev, *Spirit and Reality*, p. 141.

7. *Ibid.*, p. 142.

8. *Ibid.*

9. Georges Florovsky, "The Ethos of the Orthodox Church,"
The Ecumenical Review, 1960, p. 195.

10. Regarding Taizé, see Malcolm Boyd, "The Taizé Community," *Theology Today*, Vol. XV, No. 4 (1959), pp. 488–506.

11. Dionysios, Metropolitan of Trikka and Staghi, "The
Holy Mountain in Gratitude and Appreciation," *Sobornost'*,
Series 4, No. 10 (1964), pp. 561–562.

12. *Ibid.*, p. 564.

13. B. Bobrinskoy, "Prayer and Inner Life in Orthodox Tradition," *Studia Liturgica*, Vol. III, No. 1 (1964), p. 38.

14. Timothy Ware, "Between Heaven and Earth: Some
Notes on Contemporary Greek Monasticism," *Sobornost'*,
Series 4, No. 7 (1962), p. 402.

15. *Ibid.*, p. 405.

16. See A. Schmemann, "The Task of Orthodox Theology in
America Today," *St. Vladimir's Seminary Quarterly*, Vol. 10,
No. 4 (1966), pp. 180–194; and *Worship* (entire issue), Vol.
39, No. 10 (1965), which is devoted to a Protestant-Catholic
discussion on spiritual life today.

17. Pierre Teilhard de Chardin, *The Divine Milieu*, p. 51.

Index

215